VALUES OF THE INCARNATION

VALUES OF
THE INCARNATION

THE MOORHOUSE LECTURES 1931

BY THE REV.

P. A. MICKLEM, D.D.

*(Formerly Scholar of Hertford College, Oxford;
Rector of St. James', Sydney, New South Wales.)*

Philip Arthur 1876-

LONDON
SOCIETY FOR PROMOTING
CHRISTIAN KNOWLEDGE
NORTHUMBERLAND AVENUE, W.C. 2.
NEW YORK: THE MACMILLAN COMPANY
1932

Made and printed in Great Britain.

CONTENTS

INTRODUCTION.

THESE lectures, delivered in Melbourne last November, are the outcome of much pondering on the mystery of the Incarnation, and of the conviction that issues vital to human life and destiny, to-day as in the past, are bound up with its due apprehension and application. It was not for nothing that the Church of the early œcumenical Councils was so concerned to safeguard the full truth of the Person of Christ. Nor, however far the Christological controversies seem to have been fought over minor points of merely verbal importance, were they fought in vain. For with the truth of the Incarnation there lay, and still lie, not only issues of profound interest in the metaphysical sphere, but issues of vital importance in the domain of human character and achievement.

Indeed the definitions, accepted by the Great Church, in which those controversies found their outcome, did not so much provide a satisfying solution of an intellectual problem as safeguard and preserve complementary, even if apparently inconsistent, factors vital to religious experience. For the Incarnation meets and supplies the needs and claims of human life, both in its worth and in its imperfection, asserting on the one hand, through its maintenance of the complete and permanent manhood of Christ, the reality and value of all that is proper to man, yet on the other, through its equal maintenance of His full and complete Godhead, asserting the need of the correlation of man and of human life with the eternal order, if one and the other are to achieve their full perfection. It is then the union of Godhead and Manhood in the Person of Christ, a truth to which, in whatever terms it has been expressed and at whatever cost to logical consistency, the Church throughout has clung, which is the ultimate sanction and guarantee of human attainment, and of a complete and satisfying human life: and it has been and is the mission of the Catholic Church not only to safeguard the truth so given against any and every form of denial, but to apply it to the life of man and of society in its full scope and range.

It was not, then, in the interest merely of credal exactness but of human life and destiny that the Church in earlier and later times rejected in turn all such orders or systems of religion as tacitly or avowedly involved a denial of the full truth of the Incarnation. Consistently with this truth, the Church, itself the extension and embodiment of the Incarnation, both represents and proclaims an order of human life which on the one hand allows for the worth and freedom of all spheres of genuinely human interest and activity, yet at the same time will not allow that they are sufficient in themselves and apart from a higher order of spiritual reality under which they may and must be brought: and which on the other hand involves the reality and supremacy of the spiritual, yet not in isolation from the whole visible order, which it is set to penetrate and subdue.

The fatality of modern life is the rigid separation of the spheres of the secular and sacred, indeed the elevation of the secular to the entire exclusion of the spiritual. We are confronted to-day, as the greatest menace to spiritual truth and reality, with a vast and organised attempt to order the whole of human life and activity on a secular basis : and it is the calling of the Church not to remain behind its defences in jealous guardianship of its spiritual prerogative, but to essay under modern conditions, what it so largely achieved in the past, the assertion of the dominance of the spiritual over the whole domain of human life, while leaving to the various spheres of the latter that measure of autonomy which they rightly claim. For this task a beginning must be made in re-stating the truth of the Incarnation, and of the religion of which it is the ground, in terms of modern thought and modern life. It will then be for the Church to set out afresh on its primary mission, a mission in the fulfilment of which its special traditions and characteristic outlook call the Church of England to a share of particular importance, of applying the sacramental order and principle, which find their ultimate sanction in the Incarnation, over the whole field of human life and society.

London,
   June, 1932.

SYNOPSIS.

THE modern contention that a Hellenic and Asiatic origin is to be regarded as the basis of primitive Christianity has been largely disproved: and it is now generally acknowledged that the historical background of the doctrine of Christ and of the early Church is to be found rather in Hebraic than in non-Jewish sources. Behind the truth and outcome of the Incarnation stands the Old Testament and its historical record of the relations of God and man. The God of the prophets is a transcendent moral Person, on the one hand remote and awful in His Holiness, on the other reaching down to men with healing and redemptive grace. Over against God stands the people of God, called to reflect in their own life the righteousness and holiness of God, their first response being that of a social life ordered on principles of justice and mercy, but summoned also to a life of worship centred in the Temple and its sacrificial system. The history of Israel, in its central stream, is that of successive acts of self-transcendence, by which the people "passed over" to new and higher levels of life and consecration. Yet the destiny of Israel, as of humanity, could not be achieved by human effort or action only. There was needed also a divine initiative and a "passing over" of God to the human side.

I. THE INCARNATION AND THE OLD TESTAMENT.

THE Old Testament represents the historical setting and background of the New, and of the religion, of the origins of which the New Testament is the classical record. It is to the Old Testament, and not elsewhere, that we must turn for the history of the growth of that conception of the relation of God to man and to the whole created order, of which the Incarnation is the supreme and ultimate vindication. The unique place filled by the Old Testament in the emergence and shaping of Christianity and of the Christian conception of God has tended in recent years to be obscured through the interest aroused by the study of comparative religion, and not least by the light so abundantly thrown on the mystery cults prevalent in the Græco-Roman Empire. It need not and cannot, of course, be questioned that not within the limits of Israel only was there a *praeparatio evangelica,* that Greece, Rome and the East had their part to play in providing those conditions, that "fulness of time" which formed the occasion of the Incarnation and of the religion of the Incarnation. A further contention has however in recent years been made that the religion of the primitive church derived its shaping tendencies in the main from non-Jewish sources. Scholarly efforts have been made to interpret the early development of the doctrine of Christ, and of the faith and practice of the primitive Christian Church, as the outcome in the main of Asiatic and Hellenic conceptions and terminology. Even S. Paul, it is maintained, in his presentation of Christ and of the distinctive beliefs and ordinances of Christianity, brought in alien non-Jewish Greek ways of thought and expression, and in order to commend the Gospel to the non-Jewish, Græco-Roman world, in which he did his work, re-formed, almost re-founded, Christianity, by placing it in a setting of thought and language derived from the Græco-Roman world of his time.

The school of thinkers, who in this way seek to prove a predominantly Hellenic influence in the shaping of primitive Christianity, are thus led to set in sharp contrast the Epistles and the Gospels, at least the synoptic gospels, the exalted, reigning and worshipped Christ of the former, and the Jesus, the Prophet of Nazareth, of the latter, and to regard the epistles and the presentation of Christ which they contain as a departure, due to alien influences, from the simplicity of the Gospel. To these influences, non-Jewish and Hellenic, they ascribe the language applied to Christ and the cult of Christ, and the forms taken by the development of the doctrine and practice of primitive Christianity. It is, however, not too much to say that the main contentions of this group of scholars have been largely disproved, and that it has come to be increasingly recognised that while liberal use was made of current Greek terminology, religious and philosophical, in presenting the Gospel for the acceptance of the Greek-speaking world, yet a Jewish and not a Greek origin should in the main be sought for the religious ideas which the Apostolic writers endeavour to convey in the language which they use. " It is, I think, reasonable to conclude," writes Dr. Rawlinson, " that any fruitful examination of S. Paul's doctrine of the Person of Christ must proceed upon the assumption that its presuppositions are not syncretistic and distinctly pagan, but Jewish and Christian, and that the supposed cleavage between the Christianity of Palestine and that of the Gentile Christian Church is a chimera." [1] It may still then be affirmed, with due allowance for all the light shed on gospels and epistles alike from non-Jewish sources, that " the New Testament lies hid in the Old," and that it is to the Old Testament that we must turn for that record of religious development which culminated in the Incarnation and provided the regulative thoughts and terms with reference to God, man and the created order which underlie the religion of the Incarnation.

This fact was, of course, early recognised by the Church. It accepted the canon of the Old Testament as its own Scriptures, and used it as such long before it had its own apostolic collection of sacred writings. Indeed, from the first, the Church saw itself as the rightful heir, possessor and interpreter of the Old Testament. In Christ, believed in and worshipped, it possessed the master key to the interpretation of those scriptures. Indeed, it was itself the New Israel in and for whom the purpose and promises of God given by the prophets were to receive fulfilment.

[1] *New Testament Doctrine of the Christ,* p. 107.

New Testament writers freely drew upon the Old Testament for corroboration of their narratives and teaching. There is indeed good evidence that collections of Testimonia were formed and circulated, passages, regarded as Messianic predictions, removed from their context and arranged and published for use in Christian Apologetic. Indeed it may be said that the use of the Old Testament for purposes of corroborating the New has prevailingly taken the form of reference to proof texts rightly or wrongly regarded as Messianic. It is not, however, in isolated Messianic passages or predictions that the historical background of the Incarnation and of the religion of the Incarnation is alone or mainly to be sought. Rather must the Old Testament be taken as a whole, and viewed as that record of divine revelation, of growth in the knowledge of God and of God's relation with man, which had for its outcome and crown the Incarnation and its extension in the life of the Church. Modern critical research, and the adoption of the historical method of approach, has in this wider aspect largely enhanced the value of the Old Testament in relation to the religious development of mankind and has revealed the wisdom of the Church in adopting and retaining the Old Testament as an integral part of its own canon of scripture.

It is now viewed as a record of the age-long process by which more primitive and debased conceptions of God, His character and relations with man, yielded to those higher and more spiritual. More particularly it tells the story of a process by which, under the guidance of Israel's seers, mystics and prophets, interpreting their own experience and the events of the national life in terms of God, the thought of God as a tribal or national deity, pitted against others of like quality, gave place to the pure rich monotheism of Israel's greatest teachers. It was they who worked out, each in terms of his own age and its language and thought, those higher conceptions of God and of God's relation to man which find fulfilment in Christ and the Catholic Church. It is then to the prophetic revelation of God, His nature and dealings with man, rather than particular texts or passages selected indiscriminately from the whole range of the sacred writings, that we must look for the historical antecedents and presuppositions of the Incarnation and of all that flowed from it. It cannot be too strongly maintained that the religion of the Church derives from a far older source than the period and events of the New Testament. In Christ and in the Christian Church there is rendered explicit and carried to completion the truth of God in relation to man already embodied, or at least shadowed forth, in the Old Testament. The Israel of the New Covenant is continuous with that of the Old: and the revelation of God and the ideal of human life which reached final expression in the New Testament are in line with and emerge from the teaching of the Old, given by " divers portions and in divers manners."

The value, in relation to the main subject, of a preliminary lecture devoted to the Old Testament is twofold. It should serve on the one hand to present the Incarnation, not as an isolated historical phenomenon, nor as one related only to the Christian and Catholic religion which emerged from it, but as itself the crown, issue and fulfilment of the central stream of revelation which went before. On the other it may serve to show not only that the Old Testament is illuminated by the New, but that itself throws light upon and helps to interpret the Incarnation and the religious order based upon it. At least it may be said that no religion claiming to be final in the sense in which the religion of the Incarnation makes that claim, can vindicate itself as such unless it takes full account of, incorporates and carries to completion those facts and forms of the divine self-revelation and of man's response to that revelation which are found in the prophetic literature of the Old Testament.

Perhaps the prophetic conception of God, taken as a whole, cannot be better expressed than in the description of Him, to use A. B. Davidson's words, as a " transcendent moral person." For the term serves to state and include the twin truths, sharply contrasted, yet also mutually complementary, of the utter remoteness of God, His irresistible power, His awful holiness, and on the other hand His faithfulness and consistency in attitude and act, His condescension to man's lowliness, His mercy in redemption. Of these twin truths it is the first, that of the sole and supreme majesty of God, which received primary emphasis in the teaching of the prophets. Their insistence on this truth often indeed seems such as to be exclusive of the other and complementary one of the nearness of God to man and of the moral qualities which constitute the ground of divine action in and on the plane of human life. Yet experience shewed that in the course of religious development only one truth could find harbourage and acceptance in Israel's mind at a time. And the truth of the sole and solitary majesty of God had first to be made secure, before it could safely be modified and qualified by other aspects of the divine character. Israel lived in constant and close contact with Canaanite[2] religion and its Baal cult, a cult which identified the Deity with the local spirit and genius of fertility. It was a crude nature religion, polytheistic and non-moral, centred in local shrines each with its sacred stone and pillar conceived as the habitation of the local deity. Right up to the time of the Exile the friendly and familiar nature of the Baal cult exercised an inevitable attraction for the populace. And it was only by lifting the God of Israel into a region utterly remote from the associations of Baal worship, and setting in clear relief His supreme sole transcendent majesty, that the prophets could dissociate the God of Israel from the local nature deities and their cults, and lay the foundation of a true ethical monotheism.

In passage after passage, particularly in the later Isaiah,[3] is the sovereignty and irresistible majesty of God set forth in unqualified and uncompromising terms. And nowhere perhaps is this truth of God's absolute sovereignty brought out with greater cumu-

---

[2] See *Hebrew Religion—its origin and development,* pp. 122ff. Oesterley and Robinson.

[3] cp. Is. xl. 12ff; xliv. 6f; xlv. 21ff; xlvi. 9ff.

lative force than in the great declaration put in the mouth of God in the Book of Job (xxxviii. —xli.).   Here is, to use Dr. Otto's words, " the downright stupendousness, the well-nigh dæmonic and wholly incomprehensible character of the eternal and creative power." [4]   It is indeed the utter transcendence of God, before which man can only prostrate himself in awe and abasement, that is the primary impression made by the great outstanding theophanies, those appearances of God to men at critical moments of their lives which represent the most fateful religious experiences recorded in the Bible.   Whether in the Old Testament or indeed in the New, it is the overwhelming impression of the sole and supreme reality of God which is made at such moments.   Indeed it is precisely this aspect of the divine nature which is primarily expressed by the terms holy and holiness, the most characteristic of all the epithets applied to God by man.   Dr. Otto has brought out [5] that the divine is primarily revealed to man as the *mysterium tremendum,* as that holiness which passes understanding and in the presence of which man cannot but humble himself in utter self-abasement. Certainly for the Old Testament writers God is primarily the Holy One, " high and lifted up " above the plane of man.

And yet this remoteness of the divine from the human is a moral transcendence.   The sovereignty of God, irresistible and all-pervading, is yet not arbitrary or capricious.   It is the expression of " a constant and covenanted will."   The God of the Old

[4] *Idea of the Holy,* p. 82.   [5] *Op. cit.,* pp. 12ff.

Testament prophets is poles asunder from that non-moral absolute and arbitrary despot who is the deity of Islam. The God of the prophets reigns indeed with a complete and all-embracing sovereignty, fulfilling His own eternal purpose. His " judgments are unsearchable and His ways past finding out." His thoughts are not man's thoughts nor man's ways His. Yet He never overrides man's freedom and conscience or, in the last resort, his intelligence. His ways and doings as viewed at the time may pass man's understanding, may run counter to man's ideas of right and justice. Yet in the long run they are justified, seen to be righteous and true, and commend themselves to the higher conscience of man. This moral aspect of the divine transcendence is again brought out in those records of God's appearances to man, to which we have already alluded as the most striking examples of the sense of the awfulness and remoteness of God. The great vision of Isaiah vi. conveys the impression of a revelation of utter, dazzling holiness, before which man, nay the seraphim themselves, can but veil their faces in awe. Yet here as elsewhere man is not left in lonely, shamefaced abasement. He is bidden stand upon his feet,[6] he is called to listen to the Divine Message and to understand it, and to co-operate with the Divine will by a freely rendered obedience. He seeks and wins cleansing from his uncleanness. He is made a messenger and apostle of God with a message, heard and understood, to deliver to men. Thus God Who is utterly remote

[6] cp. Ezek. ii. 1 ; Dan. x. 10.

and highly exalted yet also draws near in utter condescension, stooping to man's weakness, setting him
on his feet, commending his ways to his understanding and his will to his freely rendered obedience.

And, on the larger scale, too, the transcendent
God is revealed as "constant and covenanted will."
It is this quality which is reflected in the term
righteousness as applied to God. His dealings with
men, even if not understood at the time, yet are
recognised as not arbitrary or capricious.   They
are marked by faithfulness and truth, maintained
through ages and generations, the rise and fall of
empires, the ups and downs of human history. The
righteousness of God, as the law of His dealings
with man, is expressed on the one hand in judgment,
the punitive discipline recognised as befalling those,
Israel or other nations, who deliberately depart in
their national or social life from the standard of
right which they recognise and have accepted; yet
also and concurrently, in redemption. Blow after
blow is struck, calamity after calamity, famine and
pestilence, defeat, captivity and exile is inflicted, but
only that He may produce that in His people's heart
which will permit Him to help and to save. He waits
only for the moment of turning, of national repent-
ance, of trust in Him, to lay bare His mighty arm in
vengeance on Israel's oppressors, in bringing again
His people from desolation or captivity, in releasing
on their behalf all the inexhaustible treasures of His
regenerative quickening healing power, in a redemption which finds expression in outward splendour and
prosperity shared in by nature as well as man.

And over against God, answering to God, the earthly counterpart of God, stands the people of God. It is not the individual, it is Israel the people which answers to God, which is the object of God's call and choice, judgments and discipline, love and redemption. It is Israel's unique rôle, as the people of God, called chosen disciplined of God, to apprehend, conserve and hand on the truth of the divine being and nature. And this witness to God and to the revealed truth of God was to be borne, not only or mainly by word of mouth or through chosen spokesmen, but in common life and by Israel as a whole. " And He said unto me, Thou art my servant; Israel, in whom I will be glorified." [7] The history of Israel is thus viewed as the training of a people under God for the unique task of manifesting in their national life the being and character of God. Israel is the chosen object and sphere of God's self-revelation, and their national mission is to reflect the truth revealed, to embody it in themselves and their common life, and to make the appropriate answer in human terms to the character of God as thus impressed upon them.

It is important to dwell for a moment on this fact of the choice of a people, and the social order and life of a people, as the object of the Divine choice, call and purpose. There is all the difference between this and the prevalent modern conception of God and the individual as being the two ultimate factors in religion, " the two only supreme and luminously self-evident beings " with whom religion is con-

[7] Is. xlix. 3.

cerned.   Nor must the conception be regarded as
merely a concession to a primitive period at which
the tribe was the unit of life, and the individual had
not attained to a status of his own.   It is true that
in the later prophetic teaching, and in the psalms
which reflect it, the individual does emerge and
occupy a responsible and privileged place in God's
sight.   Yet throughout, in the later period of the
Old Covenant as in the earlier, it remains true that
it is not the individual but Israel the people on
whom God lavishes His care and love, which is the
human answer to God's revelation and through
which He is to "break into glory."   Nor is it different
when the passage is made from the Old Testament
to the New.   The gospels and the teaching of our
Lord bring out indeed the ultimate worth of the
individual, occupied as they are to a large extent
with Christ's dealings with individual men and
women.   Yet presupposed throughout is Israel the
people, a new Israel indeed, yet continuous with the
old, and itself in its social embodiment the sphere,
channel and witness of the new order of grace.   It
is the Church which is the Body of Christ, " the
fulness of Him that filleth all in all." [8]

Thus God and His people Israel were knit together
in a covenanted and sacramental union, in which the
life of Israel was to correspond to, and to be the
visible and earthly counterpart of the nature and
character of God.   That nature and character, as
revealed through the prophets, was earlier described
as that of a " transcendent moral person " : and the

[8] Eph. i. 23.

two divine characteristics which we saw received the greatest emphasis in the prophetic writings were those of His holiness, conceived of as His transcendent otherness and remoteness from sinful man, and on the other hand of His righteousness, regarded as embodying His dealings with man, in faithfulness and truth, in judgment and redemption. Thus it was that, corresponding to the divine righteousness, the social life of Israel was to be marked by a like quality. The governing term in this connection is "chesed," usually translated mercy. It was this quality, mercy, equity, the ἐπιείκεια of the New Testament, which was attributed equally to God in His dealings with men, and to men in their dealings with each other. It was the exercise of this quality which was to be the governing principle of social life and neighbourly relationships. Corresponding to the righteousness of God there was to be a social order marked by the principle " to do justly and to love mercy." Throughout the history of Israel it is the oppression and exploitation of the poor by the rich, of the weak by the strong, and the wanton luxury resultant from it which is Israel's besetting sin : and the prophets from Amos to John the Baptist and James the brother of the Lord are at one in their denunciation of this hereditary sin and their insistence on justice and mercy between man and man. Just because God is no respecter of persons and His mercy is over all flesh, He hates robbery and oppression and the greed of gain which underlies it, and claims that between man and man which He Himself exhibits in His dealings with man.

This law of mercy in human relationships is found already in Israel's earliest codes : and the prophets of northern and southern Israel are at one in setting mercy before sacrifice as the Divine requirement. The same note is struck by John the Baptist, finds expression in our Lord's teaching and is echoed in the Epistle of James.   Thus the ethical demand which the revealed character of God makes is set in clear relief.   The social life of Israel and the dealings of Israelites with each other and with the stranger are to embody in visible and corporate form that quality of mercy which God has revealed towards man.

Thus the primary answer demanded of Israel by Israel's God lies in the ethical sphere.   It is the requirement to " do justly and to love mercy."   It is a social life answering in its governing principle to that righteousness which marks all God's dealings with man.   And it was on the ethical side of Israel's response that the insistent stress of the earlier prophets was mainly, almost exclusively, laid.   It was an insistence which went so far as, at least by comparison, a condemnation of sacrificial and ceremonial worship.   Whether in Amos, Isaiah or Micah, no language can be stronger than that used by these prophets in repudiating the meticulous observance of the sacrificial system when that observance was divorced from social justice and regard for the moral law.   But here again Israel could only learn one lesson at a time.   The Baal cult type of religion with its false conception of God and its disregard of primary moral sanctions was a constant temptation, and its inherent corruption and falsehood was only disguised when it was offered to and in the name of Jahveh. The primary demand of the God of Israel, as against the local Baals of the land, was not sacrifice but mercy: and it were better that the whole sacrificial system should go rather than that it should be regarded as a substitute for a righteous social and moral order, or as constituting in itself a guarantee of divine favour.

Yet that is not the whole story, or the whole burden of the prophetic teaching. There was another side to the religion of the Old Covenant, besides that of a right ethical relationship between man and man. The whole of religion did not consist of justice and mercy in social dealings, of primary importance though this was. It had also its Godward aspect, an aspect which found its principal corporate expression in sacrificial worship. The moral requirement once fulfilled, it must and should find its complement and climax in a ceremonial and sacrificial approach to God. And if the divine righteousness was to find its proper and necessary human counterpart in a social order based on that principle, so it was in and through its sanctuary and worship that Israel was to make its appropriate answer to the transcendent holiness of God. The ultimate demand made on Israel was that of holiness, even more than that of righteousness, just as holiness expressed more fully and finally the nature of the Divine Being. The charge " Be ye holy for I also am holy " may be regarded as Israel's supreme calling: and the protection, pledge and guarantee of a holy people answering to a holy God was primarily to be found in the sanctuary and in the law and worship of the sanctuary. Certainly from the Exile onwards it was this conception of a consecrated people, wholly dedicated to God, separated from all that was unclean, " a kingdom of priests, and an holy nation," [9] which came increasingly to dominate the religious thought and practice of the people. It had its perils, in an over-emphasis of ceremonial as compared with moral purity, in its tendency to a rigid legalism and to an undue national exclusiveness. Yet rightly conceived and carried out it was at least a stage, if not the crowning stage in the fulfilment of Israel's vocation.

The first important step towards the concentration of the national life of Israel in and on the Sanctuary, as the expression of its response to a holy God, was the discovery and promulgation of the Book of the Law in the eighteenth year of the reign of Josiah.[10] The event was followed by a thoroughgoing attempt to enforce the law so discovered and promulgated, by the cleansing of temple, city and land from idolatry, the abolition of high places and local sanctuaries, and the centralisation of all sacrificial worship in the sanctuary of the Temple. Henceforward only in Jerusalem and in the Temple might sacrifices legitimately be offered. Here was the chosen dwelling place of the God of Israel, the place where He had set His Name. Here, henceforth, the life of the people was to be centred. The set-back in the succeeding reigns and the reintro-

[9] Exod. xix. 6.   [10] B.C. 621.

duction of idolatrous worship, even the total destruction of the Temple in 587 B.C., failed to destroy the ideal thus printed on the heart of the people. The conception of the Sanctuary as the sacred centre of the nation's life and the pledge of its holiness remained, and only awaited the challenge of a prophet to be given articulate utterance and shape.

That prophet was Ezekiel, himself also a priest, and familiar with the pre-exilic temple and its ordinances. Carried captive with Jehoiakim in 597 B.C., and settled with his fellow exiles at Telabib, his prophetic work began in 592 B.C. and lasted with intermissions till 570 B.C. For him, characteristically, the primary national sin was not social injustice or wrongdoing but idolatry and the profanation of the Holy Place and objects, and his ideal was that of a regenerate and redeemed people, dedicated to God, and fulfilling its priestly service. Familiar to him was the code later than the Deuteronomic, known as the Law of Holiness,[11] a code which dealt in the main with the regulation of the Sanctuary and its worship, its prescriptions being linked with the constant refrain " Ye shall be holy; for I the Lord your God am holy." Ezekiel's call to his prophetic mission was itself preceded by a vision of God, high and lifted up, enthroned in awful holiness : and it is this vision which his prophecy seeks to translate into terms of Israel's life. In the closing section of the prophecy (xl.—xlviii.) he " presents the scheme of a politico-religious constitution in which the fundamental idea of holiness is applied to the regula-

[11] Lev. xvii.—xxvi.

tion of every part of the national life," and of which
the aim is " to maintain, on the one hand, the sanctity
of the Temple, and on the other the holiness of the
people." [12]   Careful and detailed regulations are
given as to the architecture of the Temple, its pre-
cincts and furniture, the dress, duties and revenue
of the priests, and the sacrificial worship, and all
with a view to excluding all forms of profanation
and safeguarding the holiness of God and of Israel.
I " will set My Sanctuary in the midst of them for
evermore : My tabernacle also shall be with them :
and I will be their God, and they shall be My people :
and the nations shall know that I am the Lord, that
sanctify Israel, when My sanctuary shall be in the
midst of them for evermore." [13]

For the purpose of these lectures it is perhaps
unnecessary to trace the later course of the development of the Jewish theocracy in the post-exilic
period.   It has been enough to show in the period
already covered, particularly that of creative
prophecy, that in the revelation of Godhead and
manhood which increasingly comes into view the
presuppositions of their union are already present.
This is true on the one hand on the Divine side; for
the God of the prophets is a " transcendent moral
person."   He is the " high and lofty One, that in-
habiteth eternity, whose name is Holy," yet one
who dwelleth " with him also that is of a contrite
and humble spirit." [14]   " The Lord is high above all

[12] *Introduction to the Literature of the Old Testament*
(Driver), p. 292.
[13] Ezek. xxxvii. 26ff.
[14] Is. lvii. 15.

nations : and His glory above the heavens," yet He
" humbleth Himself to behold the things that are in
heaven and in the earth." [15]   Belonging to, indeed
constituting in Himself, the eternal order, the God of
prophet and psalmist is proclaimed as " sitting above
the water flood " [16] of the changing vicissitudes of
earth and of human life.   Yet " high and lifted up "
as He is above the temporal conditions of finite man,
He yet enters into intimate relationship with man,
and submits Himself to the limiting conditions of
human life and history.   He has His own eternal
purpose to be effected on the plane and under the
limiting conditions of human life, a purpose revealed
as men can apprehend it, and carried forward as
men can co-operate with it.   He never forces the
pace beyond the capacity of man to respond.   Certainly He breaks in on man in revelations of overwhelming splendour and majesty : yet not without
man but in and through man, with all the limitations
which this involves, He carries forward His purpose
to fulfilment.   God is revealed as within the whole
course of Israel's history, sharing with His people
their vicissitudes, suffering with His people in their
calamities, bearing with His people in their follies
and sins, leading His people onward as they will
follow.   Yet equally is He not of them.   Equally is
He removed above and beyond them.   What indeed
distinguishes the God of the prophets is that He is
never the close-kept prisoner of His own world, the
pliant instrument of human planning and policy.

[15] Ps. cxiii. 4, 6.
[16] Ps. xxix. 9 (Prayer Book version).

Israel's destiny is fulfilled not in conforming God's will to theirs but in conforming their will to His, unchanging, holy and good. And it is in this very unchangeableness, in contrast with the days of man and his mortal frailty, that the hope of man lies of a destiny other than that of the grass and the beasts of the field.

So it is with the God of the prophets. In His very otherness than man, in His exalted aloofness from the plane of human life, in His unchangeableness combined with His condescension to man's weakness, His descent to man's level, lies the hope of Israel and of humanity. Yet for this there must be a response on man's side to the unchanging holiness of God, and to that gracious movement from above and beyond of revelation and redemptive grace. For on man's side, as on that of God is there in the scripture record a revelation of his nature and capacity, which represents an equally necessary pre-supposition of the union of Godhead and manhood in the person of Christ. For the record of the Old Testament in its central stream, and as interpreted by the prophets, is that of a people called from lower to ever higher levels of seeing, acting and living, and, however partially and fitfully, responding to the call. The law of Israel's calling, of Israel's life, is the law of self-transcendence, of the capacity to answer to a challenge from the other side and to make a fitting response to the divine challenge, in the concrete forms of national life and worship. Essentially, as the name suggests, the Hebrews were the people who responded at successive epochs of their history to the challenge to " pass over " to new and higher levels of character and life. The classic events of Israel's history, recalled and commemorated as such again and again in song and ballad, and in festal observance, was the passage of the Red Sea from Egypt to the Desert and to Sinai. " Till Thy people pass over, O Lord, till the people pass over which Thou hast purchased " :[17] such in the words of the Song of Moses, was the ever-renewed challenge to Israel and the hope of Israel's destiny. In themselves a people like the peoples round them, sharing their beliefs, their customs, their religion, they yet stood out in increasing distinctness from those peoples in their capacity for corporate response to the challenge which reached them from the side of God.

Very slowly they moved forward, the mass of the nation often remaining behind deaf to the higher challenge. Yet even when the many remained behind, the remnant " passed over " from the old to the new order by successive acts of renunciation and obedience. Those new and higher levels to which, in response to the divine challenge sounded through the prophets, the people were called to pass over were, as we have seen, expressed in part in social life, and in part in corporate worship. Response to the divine challenge meant in each case a new and higher standard of relationship between man and man, primarily within the limits of Israel, ultimately to include the Gentile world without, a relationship of which justice and mercy were the prevailing law. It meant, too, a directly Godward response in the

[17] Ex. xv. 16.

worship of the Temple, in which ever anew the nation dedicated itself to God and brought the whole of its life into sacrificial union with God. Moreover, those new and higher levels from which the natural man recoiled, but to which Israel or a remnant of Israel passed over, were striven for and attained not merely in deference to an impulse from within but to a challenge from without, recognised as having a compelling claim on their allegiance.

Thus in the history of Israel was illustrated through the medium of events and their interpretation by the prophets the capacity of man for reaching beyond himself towards a higher and eternal order in which alone he could find rest but yet which by his own effort he could not attain. For Israel's life is the spiritual history of humanity. The destiny of man to be taken up into fellowship with God, and the stages by which that destiny is achieved, are symbolised in the great passages of Israel's life from Egypt to the desert, from the desert to Canaan, from Palestine to the Captivity of Babylon, from Babylon back to their own land. These historic events in Israel's chequered record represented the outward embodiment of those successive acts of self-transcendence by which in response to the divine challenge the people of God fulfilled its calling, to be a " holy people " and the dwelling-place of God. Yet the hope of Israel, and through Israel of humanity, could not be attained by human response alone. The ground could be prepared for a further and final act of self-transcendence by increasing receptiveness of the divine challenge. In this lay a necessary condition of man's crowning achievement, not that achievement itself. Man could only reach out hands to a goal which yet ever eluded him. The initiative must be taken by God. God must " pass over " to the human side if man's goal was to be reached, and his capacity for self-transcendence was to achieve its crowning triumph : and in Jesus, " born of a woman, born under the law," that passage was taken by a culminating act of divine self-limiting and condescension, of which the conditions were present in an utter receptiveness on the human side. Thus the " Word made flesh " in the Person of Jesus Christ is the final outcome of the revelation of God-head and manhood, and of the relation between God and man, given in historical form and interpreted in the Scripture record.

SYNOPSIS.

THE Gospels are to be regarded not as the one source of a true doctrine of Christ, but as providing a test and ultimate standard of any such formulated doctrine : at the same time, no such doctrine can be adequate which fails to do justice to the Gospel record. The doctrine of Christ took shape in the early Church as the interpretation of Christian experience, of what Christ was found to be in the experience of the individual and of the Church. Behind the teaching of S. Paul is his own vivid experience of redemption and re-creation in Christ. With S. John it is rather an experience of revelation and of fellowship, from which his teaching of the Christ springs. In formulating the doctrine of Christ the Church was primarily concerned not to reach conclusions satisfying to logical consistency, but to safeguard the religious values found to be bound up with the Incarnation. It rejected heresies because in one respect or another they failed to do justice to those values. Such was Apollinarianism with its denials of the completeness of Christ's human nature. Such was Nestorianism with its denial to Christ of whole and complete Godhead. The value of the Chalcedonian definition was not that of providing a formula ultimately satisfying to human thought, but of safeguarding those truths of Christ's Person which were involved in Christian experience and embodied in the Gospel portrait. The Christ of the Gospel record is both human and divine.

II. THE INCARNATION IN THE EARLY CHURCH.

No doctrine of Christ and of the Incarnation can be regarded as adequate which does not do full justice to the portrait of Jesus given in the Gospels. Yet it is of the first importance to estimate aright the place which the Gospels fill in reference to an adequate formulation of such a doctrine. It is indeed often maintained that it is to the Gospels, and to the Gospels alone, that we must go for materials of such a formulation. Once depart from the Gospels, so it is urged, and the truth of Christ becomes distorted and perverted through human prejudice and prepossession. And when in times resentful of dogmatic definition and indeed of institutional Christianity, the cry " Back to Christ " is raised, the meaning of such an implied protest is that, to find the true Christ, we must go back behind the Church and the Creeds, behind the centuries of doctrinal development through which the Church passed, back to the Gospels and to the Christ of the Gospels, and, without any bias or presupposition, seek there for the unvarnished truth.

The tendency, natural and indeed inevitable though it may be at certain times, is yet one which involves a rejection of the corporate experience of the Christian community as entering into a right formulation of the truth as it is in Jesus. It implies and indeed often states that with the period of

ecclesiastical controversy and definition, indeed with
S. Paul himself, there occurred a decisive turning
away from the originality of the Gospel record, and
the simple truth of the Christ there to be found, to
the barren task of word-splitting and disputation.
Those who would know the real Christ, so it is maintained, must find Him, if at all, not in the Church
and its corporate experience as formulated in the
Creeds and conciliar definitions, not even in the
Pauline letters which are the outcome of such experience, but in the Gospels, and particularly in the
synoptic Gospels, and there only. Hence occur those
interpretations of the Christ, formed on what claims
to be an unprejudiced examination of the Gospel
records, with which for long past we have been made
familiar and which are still attempted. From such
researches and their literary outcome there emerges
a Christ very different from the Christ of Christian
experience, as expressed in creed and worship. Just
a century ago, Strauss was but the forerunner of a
number of writers who, by the simple process of
eliminating from the Gospels elements essential to
them, have presented us with a Christ from the
Person of whom all traces of the supernatural and
transcendent are carefully removed. The history of
these attempts to find the real Christ by a simple
return to the Jesus of the Gospels, and the conclusion
so reached, have been ably reviewed in his well
known book *The Quest of the Historical Jesus,* by
Albert Schweitzer, who, by recoil from the non-
miraculous Christ of his predecessors, has discovered
in the Gospels the apocalyptic Messiah, careless of

and indifferent to the existing order, and only intent on the miraculous, God-given consummation of the age to be inaugurated at His own second coming.

The outcome of the endeavours to re-discover the real Christ and to formulate a true doctrine of Christ by this method has been to show conclusively that it leads, and can lead, to no satisfactory result, valuable service though it has rendered in bringing into clear prominence elements in the Gospels which had been ignored or lost to sight. The conclusions of such attempts are only reached by isolating and giving undue prominence to special features of the Gospel portrait of Christ, at the cost, however, of ignoring and even denying the existence of other factors. Such researches then are not so scientifically unprejudiced as they claim to be. Indeed, their conclusions can generally be shown to be the result of a strong prepossession in the writer or his age. Thus, for example, the non-miraculous Christ of Strauss and Renan was the Christ congenial to an optimistic age of progress and enlightenment and scientific discovery in which man was regarded as sufficient for himself : while the visionary Christ of eschatology is the reflection of a strain or period of pessimism, despairing of the world and of human nature, and seeing no hope but in the miraculous intervention of God, and in the passing of the present evil age and the divine inauguration of a new.

The inference, however, to be drawn from the failure of such attempts to reach an adequate and satisfying doctrine of Christ, by going behind the formulated experience of the Church back to the

Gospel record, is not, of course, that the Gospels have no place to fill in the history of Christian doctrine. It is rather to show that the attempts in question are based on a wrong conception of the place, an indispensable one, which the Gospels alone can fill in relation to the doctrine of Christ and the Incarnation. Historically, of course, the Gospels were not the source from which the Church derived its belief in Christ. Rather is it true to say that the Gospels emerged from the heart of a believing and worshipping Church. The need for a Gospel record, indeed for a succession of such records, arose at successive stages of the Apostolic period in a Church which already believed, already worshipped, and was already constructing its credal basis. The service which the Gospels were designed to render was not then that of providing material out of which the Church's belief about Christ could be formulated, but that of providing the test and ultimate standard of reference for any such formulation.

Very early the need arose for giving written shape to the historical background of the life, belief and worship of the Church. Indeed, the Gospels met, and may well have been deliberately designed to meet, the peril of forgetting that historical background, and of so concentrating on the glorified Christ of Christian worship and experience as to lose sight of the identity of the Christ whom they worshipped with the historical person of Jesus of Nazareth. It would be a crude way of putting it to say that the Christian communities of the Apostolic age were so absorbed in the divine Christ as to

forget the human.   Yet the peril of a docetic view
of Christ, with all its consequences in the moral
sphere, was there, as repeated warnings show : and
on one side at least the Gospels may be said to have
supplied a needed corrective to the natural tendency
of a living, growing, worshipping Christian community to concentrate only on a heavenly Christ, and
to forget the earthly Jesus and the days of His Flesh.
The Gospels, then, and their portrait of Jesus emerge
from a believing and worshipping Church, and were
composed[1] in response to successive demands at
particular centres, in order to place on permanent
written record the historical events which formed
the inalienable background of the faith and practice
of the Church, and in so doing to provide a test and
standard by which any doctrine of Christ which
sought for recognition could stand or fall.

The Gospels thus represent a fundamental
standard of reference for the Church's formulated
doctrine of Christ : nor can any such doctrine be
regarded as acceptable which fails to do justice to
the Gospel record.   There is, however, another
standard of reference, final in a sense in which even
the Gospels are less than final.   For, as we have seen,
the Gospels themselves are the product of a believing
and worshipping Church, of a community living the
Christian life.   They are the outcome of the experience, fresh living and growing, of the Apostolic
Church, and they present the figure of Jesus and the
story of His life as looked at and reflected in the
mirror of that experience.   They are interpretations

[1] See *The Four Gospels:* Streeter, pp. 9ff.

of the Christ of corporate experience rather than detached biographical studies. Of the fourth Gospel this is obviously and pre-eminently true : but it is true in its measure also of the synoptic Gospels, each of which represents a viewpoint and interpretation of the Christ as characteristic of and appealing to a particular *milieu* of Christian corporate life. Bishop Hart [2] has recently pointed out that even S. Mark is not the naïve chronicle of events often supposed but is a presentation of Jesus from certain aspects and for certain purposes. This truth in no way detracts from the historical value of the Gospels. It only serves to bring into clearer prominence the fact that behind the New Testament as a whole, including the Gospels, is the life of fellowship, faith and worship lived by the Christian community, and that the New Testament as a whole, including the Gospels, is the outcome of the corporate experience of the Church. True it is that the New Testament canon of Scripture, once formed and accepted as the authentic record of the Christian experience of the Apostolic age, became separated off as the accepted norm and touchstone of later formulations of doctrine. Yet for the New Testament, including the Gospels, as for later interpretations of the Christ, the determinant and shaping factor is that which Christ was found to be in the living experience of the Christian Church : and just as the prophets of the Old Covenant read their teaching of God into and out of the events, national and personal, of their time, so the Christ of the New Testament and of the

[2] *The Gospel Foundations* (Moorhouse Lectures, 1928).

Catholic creeds was the outcome and interpretation of the Christ of both personal and corporate experience. The doctrine of the Christ, then, as it gradually took shape in the Apostolic age and later, was an interpretation of His Person in such available terms as were least inadequate to what in actual experience Christ was found to be. That experience, as it became increasingly conscious of itself, recognised certain ultimate religious values as bound up with Christ : and no formula which purported to analyse or define His Person, however apparently self-consistent and logical, could hope to secure final acceptance, the logical consistency of which was purchased at the cost of excluding any such religious value.

Such was pre-eminently the case with the doctrine of Christ's Person as adumbrated by S. Paul. That doctrine emerged from and was the formulated interpretation of his own very vivid and sharp-cut religious experience. The Christ of S. Paul was the Jesus who had appeared to him " in the way," the Christ of the divine act, redemptive and creative, by which his own life had been cut in two, by which he had " passed over " from an old to a new order of existence, an act, in one sense, of a historic moment in the past and clearly remembered, yet, in another, present and continuous. That revelation had been for him one, from without and from beyond, of a transcendent and glorified Lord. Yet, transcendent as the experience was, it had not crushed or obliterated his individuality. It was creative rather than destructive. Henceforth he lived his life " in Christ," and through the Christ, transcendent yet also indwelling, constituted henceforth as the centre and heart of his being, he had come to himself and attained the full measure of his manhood.   It was thus a keen, vivid sense of forgiveness, of moral emancipation, of life lived henceforth on a new and higher level to which he had attained in Christ, an experience, moreover, derived directly from, and made possible by, the death and resurrection of Jesus.

Moreover, that experience, though intensely personal, was not peculiar to him.   It was typical and representative.   He could appeal to others for testimony to a like redemption.   A like faith in Christ, a like experience of Christ, was common to the whole company of believers.   It was on the basis of a common salvation that their fellowship was established : and it was as the intellectual interpretation of this redemptive re-creative experience, shared by him and the whole body of believers, that S. Paul formulated his representative statements of the doctrine of Christ's Person.   In the most characteristic of these [3] it is noticeable how the formulation of the doctrine of Christ's Person, both in relation to the Church and to the created order as a whole, occurs in closest connection with a reference to a common experience of deliverance and new life, of forgiveness and redemption, found in Christ.   It is in the light of that experience that Christ is declared not only as head of the new order of the Church, but also as head of the old order of nature, " the

[3] Coloss. i. 15ff.

First-born who is at the same time the first principle
of all things, the Architype of the created universe,
the Intermediary of God in creation, the source, goal
and sustainer of the world as created." [4]   Thus for
S. Paul Christ stands pre-eminent, above and beyond
the natural order and man as the final term of that
order, yet also in intimate relation with it and with
him, redeeming, reconstituting in Himself not
humanity only but the whole world of nature to
which humanity belongs.   Yet however far-reaching
in its metaphysical implications is the doctrine of
Christ as so formulated, in the last resort it is but
the expression in such terms as were available, borrowed in the main it would seem, not from Greek
but from Jewish terminology, of that experience of
Christ, redemptive, regenerative, recreative, which
S. Paul shared with the Christian community as a
whole.

   With S. John the emphasis alters.   The sharpcut
divisive experience of a S. Paul is lacking.   The
settled order of the life of fellowship and contempla-
tion has taken its place.   The characteristic earlier
terms, redemption and reconciliation, fall into the
background : and another set of terms, beholding,
knowledge, vision and revelation, take their place.
For S. John the Christ is the " Word made Flesh,"
the absolute revelation of God in terms of humanity.
In Christ he had " beheld His glory, glory as of the
only-begotten from the Father." [5]   His approach to
truth is sacramental.   In Christ he sees man and the

---

[4] *New Testament Doctrine of Christ* (Rawlinson), p. 161.
[5] Jn. i. 14.

world of men transfigured by contact with the
Divine. It is with this vision in view, of Christ as
the revelation of the Divine in terms of the human,
that the incidents and order of the Fourth Gospel
are selected and arranged. Each incident in turn is
intended to declare and unveil some aspect of the
Eternal through the temporal setting given to it.
Hence the marriage feast of Cana is set first among
the signs of Jesus, because in an outstanding way it
was typical of that manifestation of His glory[6]
which was the object of His mission and ministry.
Even the Passion narrative is told primarily from
this standpoint. The " lifting-up from the earth " of
Christ is interpreted as the crowning act of divine
self-revelation even more than as one of redemption
and reconciliation. And such for S. John was that
revelation of the divine which Christ embodied and
conveyed that, while given from within the order of
human life, it could only be given by One who
Himself also stood outside and beyond that order
and was one with God. The character of the
revelation made was such as to demand a correspondingly absolute character in the Revealer. None but
" the only-begotten Son, who is in the bosom of the
Father "[7] could " declare Him " as Christ had revealed God. It is the same conclusion, drawn from
a unique religious experience, which underlies the
Logion of Jesus found in the synoptists : " Neither
doth any know the Father save the Son, and he to
whomsoever the Son willeth to reveal him."[8] So the

[6] Jn. ii. 11.   [8] Mth. xi. 27. Cp. Lk. x. 22.
[7] Jn. i. 18.

Christ of S. John, sharing to the full the nature and conditions of humanity, yet stands on the Divine side. He is one with the Father whom with final and adequate assurance he declares and reveals : and the whole purpose of the Gospel is to drive home the absolute and final character of that sonship which belongs to one who had revealed God as Christ had revealed Him.

A like conclusion as to the Person of Christ emerges from yet another aspect of Christian experience, characteristic of S. John and the Johannine writings, that of fellowship, the fellowship of members of the beloved community with Christ, and in Christ with one another, a fellowship which can only be interpreted as the reflection in human terms of an eternal fellowship within the being of God. The First Epistle was avowedly written in the light of that experience of fellowship with and in Christ, written to deepen and enlarge that fellowship and to declare its divine origin and source. The revelation which Christ made was, above all, one of divine love, of God as love, a love which was reflected and embodied in the life of the beloved community. The fellowship so known and experienced was of a different order from any fellowship constituted on a solely human basis. It belonged already to the eternal sphere. Those who were of it had already passed out of death into life. But if such was the rich experience of fellowship in the redeemed community mediated by Christ, it was seen that that earthly fellowship must be grounded in the very being of God. It must " derive from an eternal order of love." Thus the Christ through whom this new and higher order of human fellowship is realised belongs Himself to an eternal and divine order of fellowship. " The fellowship, or κοινωνία of the Spirit in the new Community is referred back to a transcendent fellowship of Persons in the life of God." [9] Yet here again the conclusion so reached emerged from the background of a concrete human experience. It was the knowledge of the Christ " loving His own and loving them to the end," of the Christ bidding His disciples keep the new commandment of love, it was the experience of that love embodied and expressed in the life of the Church's brotherhood which drove S. John to predicate behind it an eternal order of love and to see in Christ One who " from the beginning " was " with God " and " was God."

Already then in the Apostolic age it was Christian experience which largely determined the formulation of Christian doctrine : and in particular the place and titles assigned to Christ were primarily such as were necessitated by what in experience, the corporate experience of the Church, He had been found to be. And here, too, in the religious values and interests associated with Christ and experienced by the Christian community, was the determinant factor which guided the Church through the era of Christological discussion and controversy which culminated with the promulgation of the Chalcedonian formula in A.D. 451. The supreme value of the latter, with its insistence on the unity of Christ's

[9] *The Incarnate Lord:* Thornton, p. 305.

Person, a unity which yet included the reality and permanence of each nature, was not that it provided a definition ultimately satisfactory to human thought, but that it authoritatively preserved those factors, the sacrifice of any one of which, however far it subserved the demands of logical consistency, would have done violence to that whole of religious experience of which the doctrine was an attempted explanation. This is not to assign to Christian doctrine a purely pragmatic value, or to make practical demands a test of truth. Ultimately indeed a doctrine of Christ's Person must be satisfying to human thought, as well as adequate to religious experience. Yet just as no scientific generalisation proves acceptable to the scientific world, unless it includes and allows for all the relevant data, so the data of Christian experience, in revelation and redemption, in worship and fellowship, must be included in, or at least not excluded by, any doctrine of the Person of Christ which is set forth for general acceptance.

Reasons will be given later for the view that modern categories of thought are more adequate than ancient to provide a mould within which a philosophically satisfying doctrine of the Incarnation can take shape. Meanwhile, it will be well to return to the period of the Councils, the period at which the subject of the Person of Christ was paramount in Christian thought and apologetic. An examination of the period, even in briefest outline, will be sufficient to show that the Great Church was primarily concerned not to reach a logically complete and consistent statement of doctrine, but to safeguard the ultimate religious values which were bound up with the Incarnation and the Person of Christ, as against any endeavours at precise definition which, however attractive to abstract thought, were yet calculated to endanger or undermine those values. " The heresies were not excluded because their use of terminology was less scientific or exact than that of orthodox theologians." [10] They were excluded because of " their incompatibility with religious interests," [10] and their inadequacy to the fulness of religious experience.

Such was the case with Apollinarianism. Here was the attempt of a great thinker and religious genius to safeguard the transcendent and divine in the Person of Christ, without surrendering its unity. As against the Christ of Arianism, neither god nor man, Apollinaris was concerned to assert the full divinity of Christ as an essential implication of Christian experience. He was fundamentally right in thus affirming a truly and fully divine Christ. For no other could be adequate to what in the experience of the Church Christ had been found to be. Yet he found no means of securing this fundamental truth except that of surrendering another equally fundamental. To him, as to the general thought of his day, Christian and non-Christian alike, the divine and the human were separated as " two ultimately antipathetic " entities, inherently incompatible the one with the other. A priori Godhead and manhood were cut off the one from the other by an unbridged and unbridgeable gulf, the Godhead impassible,

[10] Thornton, op. cit., p. 254.

changeless and infinite, manhood inherently finite,
sinful, subject to vicissitude.   How then could room
be found for both in the Person of Christ?   If the
two natures were both present, there must be two
Persons, two Christs.   For a complete nature involved a complete personality. One then or the other
must be sacrificed to the paramount need of securing
the unity of Christ's Person.   Religious experience,
especially in its characteristically eastern tendencies,
demanded in Christ a full expression of the Divine.
Humanity then, or at least that element of manhood
which rendered it inherently incompatible with union
with the Divine, must be surrendered.   Hence the
Apollinarian teaching that " the place of the human
nous was taken by the divine immutable and infallible
Logos, who as the ruling principle secured for the
humanity of Christ immunity from just those weak-
nesses, just that liability to creaturely vicissitudes,
which in other men followed from their possession
of a human nous." [11]   Thus account was taken of the
axioms of human thought accepted at the time; and
the divine in Christ was secured, as the factor which
was primary to the whole of Christian experience,
but only at the cost of surrendering another equally
fundamental factor : and in A.D. 362 Apollinarianism
was   condemned   because " the   completeness of
Christ's human nature was impaired, and as a
consequence, the whole redemption wrought by
Christ was defective." [12]

    This is not the place to discuss whether Apollinaris

[11] *A Study in Christology:* Relton, p. 9.
[12] *op. cit.,* p. 12.

was not greater than his critics and his disciples, and whether the divine Logos for which he claimed room at any cost in the Person of Christ, so far from removing and diminishing, did not actually supply just that element of perfect manhood, which otherwise would have been lacking. It is enough to point out that, if not Apollinaris himself, then the system of thought which goes by his name, was a marked concession to the pantheistic tendencies characteristic of Oriental thought and of Oriental religion and practice. Certainly, as carried further in the teaching of Eutyches and in the popular cult of Monophysitism, it was a denial and surrender of elements of religious experience which rightly claimed recognition. It provided the theological background of that religious attitude, which has for its ideal the merging of the individual in God, the absorption of the human in the divine. It was wholly right in its assertion that manhood could not reach completion or consummation in its own right and within its own limits, that manhood could only attain its goal by being taken to God. It was wrong in its presupposition that this consummation could only be attained by denying to manhood, as so assumed, a continuance of its own proper nature and its own law of being. " Christian thought does not lead us to believe that the future holds for us the destruction of our human nature, but its final and complete purification and restoration." [13] For human nature, however in itself partial and incomplete, has its own inalienable value : and no solution of the

[13] *op. cit.,* p. 40.

problem of man's relation to God is adequate which constitutes a denial or forfeiture of that value. " Human life is neither simply autonomous and self-completing, nor is it doomed to be frustrated by some higher order of existence.   Its destiny is that it should be completed in God." [14]   In condemning Apollinarianism, in declaring Monophysitism a heresy, in asserting the perfect Manhood of Christ, the Church repudiated the view, ultimately deriving from the Oriental conception of the visible world as evil if not unreal, " that the entry of the divine into human life must involve in some degree a superseding of the full and free manifestation of what belongs to the domain of the human spirit." [15]   We shall trace out later some of the practical implications of this tendency of thought and practice which have appeared in history, and are far from non-existent at the present day.   For it is, as we shall see, from this wrong conception of the Incarnation that are ultimately derived those systems of thought and practice which so far assert the primacy of the spiritual as to deny or belittle the material, and press the specifically religious aspect of life so far as to override and deny scope to those legitimate expressions of the human spirit for which room must be found in a complete human life, indeed in a complete religion.   Hence the need apprehended and asserted by the Church of holding to the reality and permanence of the manhood of Christ.

Over against the school of thought and practice

[14] *The Incarnate Lord:* Thornton, p. 265.
[15] *op. cit.,* p. 264.

centred in Egypt at Alexandria, oriental in origin, pantheistic and mystical in tendency, looking for the merging of the human in the divine as the ideal of life, is that represented by Antioch and Syria, with its " opposed conceptions which endeavoured to do justice to the dignity and worth of human nature." [16] In a very real sense it embodies a justifiable protest against a natural tendency, found already within the Apostolic age, to sublimate the Christ to a region which rendered His humanity illusory and unreal : and we have seen how, on one side, the Gospels themselves represent a redressing of the balance in their life story of the man Christ Jesus, and their emphasis, an emphasis equally pronounced in the fourth Gospel as in the Synoptists, on the human traits and limitations of Jesus. It was at Antioch however and in the Antiochean school of theology that the truth of the real and complete humanity of Christ received its most marked and indeed its exaggerated expression. The doctrinal tendency of this school runs back at least to the later years of the third century and to the patriarchate of Paul of Samosata (A.D. 260—270). The school which looked to him as its founder " allowed no difference in kind between the indwelling of the Logos in Christ and in any human being, only one of degree, the Logos having dwelt and operated in Him after a higher manner than in any other man." [17] Thus Christ is represented as earning His Godhead, and as becom-

---

[16] *Encyclopædia of Religion and Ethics* (Hastings), Vol. I., p. 593.

[17] Murray's *Dictionary of Christian Biography,* p. 816.

ing worthy of union with God by progressive development from below.

It is, however, with Nestorius, more than a century later, and with the heresy rightly or wrongly associated with his name, that this adoptionist view of the Person of Christ attained its most marked prominence.   Into the implications of the term Theotokos, on which the Nestorian controversy turned, there is no need to enter.   Here it is sufficient to point out that the denial of that title to Christ was the corollary of the presupposition, common to the Antiochean school, of approaching the problem of the Person of Christ from the human side, and of finding room for the divine in Christ only so far as was compatible with a real and complete manhood : a presupposition at the back of which lay the rightful insistence on religious values of primary importance.

For here, too, the determinant factor was the compelling need of finding room for religious values equally fundamental with those asserted by the Apollinarian school in any doctrine of Christ which could claim general recognition.   Yet here again the conceptual axioms of the day demanded the sacrifice of His full and complete Godhead as the price of asserting His full and complete manhood.   For with a human nature inevitably went, so it was assumed, a human personality.   If Christ then was truly and completely man, He could not also be truly and completely God :   or in so far as He was also God, there could be no real union.   There was a division of person; in fact, not one, but two Christs.   Here, however, was a conclusion wholly unacceptable.

Christ, then, it was inferred, was a man in whom the
Logos dwelt in a pre-eminent degree who received
of the Spirit without measure, " a perfect human
individual who is filled to the full with divine life
and power : " and His divinity was conceived of in
terms of moral value and capacity to mediate a
supreme revelation of God. Room was thus found
in the Person of Christ for the divine only as a
moral indwelling of the Spirit of God, in a supreme
degree indeed, yet not different in kind from
that which is possible and is experienced in
the case of men generally. Thus Nestorianism is
the parent of those systems of adoptionism which
picture Christ as a man raised to the status of Son
of God and endued in supreme degree by the Spirit
of God and so fulfilling His mission to mankind.

It is obvious how clearly allied is this view of the
Incarnation and of the religion based upon it with
prominent tendencies in present-day thought. Yet
over against the Monophysite school, that of Antioch
rendered an invaluable service in the cause of religious truth. It was a " splendid vindication of the
historical Christ . . . and the historical portrait in
the Gospels." [18] It asserted certain ultimate religious
interests. It insisted at any cost on finding room for
a full humanity in the Person of Christ and for the
permanence of that manhood after the Incarnation.
It thus stood for the inalienable right of human
nature, and with it of the created world, to full
recognition as of ultimate value, and as finding a
place in any order of life which rested on Christ's

[18] *A Study in Christology: Relton,* p. 21.

Person.   It asserted that no religion was adequate
to human needs which did not allow for the claims
of human individuality and of all that properly
belonged to the domain of the human spirit.   Yet in
this rightful assertion Adoptionism lost sight of that
other equally essential religious interest on which
the opposing school laid equally exclusive stress.   It
ignored in the sphere of religion the fact that human
nature, with all its claim to full recognition, yet
could not within its own limits attain its goal.
Human nature in itself is stamped with the mark of
non-attainment.   Nor can a Christ who, however
far divinely inspired and endowed, yet remains
within the limits of the organic order of human life,
be adequate to human need.   It is only as He stands
above and beyond the organic order, and on the
level of the eternal, that Christ can be a final revelation of God to man.   As a perfect man there is not
that in Him which is unique :   there is continually
the possibility of another to stand beside Him in His
character as revealer of the divine. Still less is man's
need of redemption supplied by One who is of the
same order of life and being as mankind generally :
and if the needs of redemption claim that in the
Christ there should be whole and complete manhood, it claims equally that there should be in Him
that which is whole and complete Godhead, reaching
down from above and beyond and fulfilling that in
and for man which man in his own strength is
inadequate to do for himself.

The long period of Christological debate and
definition reached a halting point with the Council

of Chalcedon, A.D. 451, and with the formula which it enunciated and promulgated. Its task and its achievement was in no sense to provide an ultimate solution of the mystery of Christ's Person. It was content to recognise the mode of the Incarnation as "ineffable and inconceivable," a mystery baffling human comprehension. Its supreme value lay in the authoritative stamp which it set, at whatever risk of the charge of self-contradiction, on the correlative truths of the unity of Christ's Person, and of the reality and permanence of each nature, human and divine. It warned the Church off the tempting paths along which Apollinarianism on the one hand and Nestorianism on the other had pointed, modes of conceiving the Incarnation which purchased logical consistency at the cost of surrendering one or other element of Christ's Person, one or other factor essential to Christian experience. Its four negative adverbs, " without confusion, without conversion, without division, without separation," were " convenient signposts, each with a warning to the traveller that he might know what to avoid in his journey as a seeker after the truth." [19] But in no sense did they, or the whole definition, preclude further investigation into the seeming contradictions of Christ's Person or further search for a solution of the problem which would be both inclusive of the data and also satisfying to human thought : and indeed the challenge of the formula was no sooner thrown down than it was taken up by Leontius of Byzantium and met by the

[19] Relton, *op. cit.*, p. 37.

doctrine of the Enhypostasia,[20] " as the only way of escape from the Nestorian and Monophysite pitfalls," a doctrine by which the attempt is made to secure the permanence and reality of Christ's Manhood within the unity of Christ's divine Person. Meanwhile, the Chalcedonian formula had not only stated the irreducible data, of which account must be taken, and for which room must be found, in any adequate doctrine of Christ's Person. Equally or even more important it had safeguarded and preserved those truths relating to the Incarnation which had been found essential to Christian experience on the one hand and to the imperishable Gospel portrait on the other. For there throughout, however *a priori* incredible, stood the fact of Christ enshrined in the historical records of the Gospels, and an ultimate test of any doctrine of Christ's Person set forth for general acceptance.

We return then, in conclusion, to the Gospels regarded, as earlier maintained, less as material of the Church's defined doctrine of Christ than as a crucial test of any such formulated statement. It cannot indeed be asserted too strongly that no doctrine of Christ and of the Incarnation can be regarded as true or sufficient which is untrue to the facts as given in the Gospels. Nor in speaking of the Gospels, as supplying an ultimate test of such a doctrine, need we or ought we to confine ourselves to the Synoptic Gospels, or to S. Mark as the basic Gospel of the three. Too often, in attempts to present the Christ of the Gospel record, has the

[20] See Relton, *op. cit.,* pp. 69ff.

synoptic and even the Markan standpoint been taken into consideration as alone of historical value for this purpose. For the human portrait of Jesus, it is maintained, we must turn to the Synoptic writers, and particularly S. Mark, the implication being that as against them the fourth Gospel provides rather an ideal mystical interpretation of the Person of Christ than a historical portrait. It is true that " the charm of S. Mark " consists very largely in the naïve ungarnished human touches of his narrative and portrait, touches which are often, it would appear, deliberately excluded from the parallel passages in S. Matthew and S. Luke. It is true also that the claims of Christ to a unique relationship with God, generally placed in His own mouth, and to qualities and functions which pronounce Him divine, are more prominent in the fourth Gospel, that indeed the Christ of the fourth Gospel is pre-eminently He at whose feet S. Thomas fell with the adoring acknowledgment " My Lord and my God." But this fact in no way involves a denial of its historical worth. For, however far the writer's aim is interpretation rather than biography, this does not alter the fact that he deliberately uses the form and outline, already recognised, of the gospel life of Jesus as the medium of his interpretation : nor again the fact, as Bishop Hart is only the latest to point out,[21] that the writer of the fourth Gospel shows a close, indeed a first-hand acquaintance with the events and personalities of his record, and again and again corrects or supplements the earlier writers on matters of

[21] *The Gospel Foundations;* Moorhouse Lectures, 1928.

historical happening, when such correction was called for. Moreover, if it be true that the interest of the fourth Gospel lies rather in interpretation than in narrative, the same may be said of the Synoptic writers, even including S. Mark, who also are primarily concerned, while using the medium of a chronicle of events carefully selected and arranged, to convey a certain impression of the significance of Christ and His mission, rather than to provide a biographical record. Nor is it true, to return to the fourth Gospel, that it presents us with a Christ removed from and above human conditions and limitations. So far is this from being the case that it is rather true that no Gospel labours more to bring into clear relief the reality of the human experiences of Jesus. He is " wearied with His journey " :[22] He is " moved with indignation in the spirit," [23] and " troubled." [24] He weeps :[25] He thirsts.[26] " Stress is laid in this Gospel to an extent which is unparalleled in the Synoptists, upon the susceptibility of Christ to purely physical and simple human experience." [27] The Gospels, then, the fourth as much as or even more than the Synoptists, are alike in presenting a Christ concerned with the here and now of everyday life, subject to human needs, susceptible to human emotions, sharing to the full the lot and circumstances of human nature.

[22] Jn. iv. 6.
[23] Jn. xi. 33.   (R.V. margin).
[24] Jn. xi. 33.
[25] Jn. xi. 35.
[26] Jn. xix. 28.
[27] *New Testament Doctrine of the Christ:* Rawlinson, p. 203.

Yet that is not the whole of the Gospel portrait, even as given by S. Mark and the other Synoptists. The Christ whom the Evangelists present is within the sphere of humanity, yet not of it. He is subject to the conditions of the created order, yet also and at the same time He transcends it, and is above and beyond it. And this impression of the Christ as " a transcendent moral person," though less prominent and outspoken in the Synoptists than in S. John, yet again and again breaks through the story and asserts itself all the more strikingly for the fact that it is not consciously or deliberately obtruded. There is an element of the above and beyond about Him, coming out in action and word, in His very appearance, which the writers do not attempt to explain yet faithfully record. The impression made by His teaching is one of amazement at the authority with which He spoke, as of One who claimed for His words an absolute and final character because He said them. The teaching is given in the colloquial tongue of his own day and people, and comes home to them with familiar force and appeal : yet in spite of the simplicity and immediacy of its appeal to its hearers, perhaps indeed because of it, it also possesses a universal character which makes it authoritative for all men and for all times. Particularly is this so with His message of the Kingdom. The term itself was familiar to His hearers as, with whatever other associations of a lower kind, that transcendent order of life and of society on which Israel's hopes were traditionally set, and by membership in which those hopes were to be fulfilled.

But while they were subjects of the kingdom, He was not subject only but King. " Our Lord speaks not as a stranger or a neophyte within the gates of the kingdom, but as one familiar with its whole territory. He speaks of that transcendent order as one who knows it from within with a familiar intimacy. . . . . He is not simply a citizen of the Kingdom giving allegiance to it. He is its King, who possessing its secret treasures can convey them to others." [28] So, too, His claim that " the Son of Man hath power on earth to forgive sins " is one which, by the testimony of His critics, is by implication a claim to be on the level of Deity. And again with His assertion of a right to be supreme and final judge of quick and dead, an assertion which we should expect to be made only " by One conscious of the absolute character of His personality in its relationship with all mankind." [29] His works of healing and exorcism are pointed to as evidence that " the Kingdom of God is come upon you," [30] that in and through Him God had intervened on the plane of human life with redeeming grace and energy. Lastly His consciousness, not seldom revealed, of a unique filial relationship with God, found not in S. John only but in the Synoptists, implies the presence of One who, while within the human and natural order of life, yet stands above and beyond it.

So the Gospels reveal Him both human and divine. Yet there is no duality about the Person so revealed.

[28] *The Incarnate Lord:* Thornton, pp. 247f.
[29] Relton, *op. cit.,* p. 258.
[30] Mth. xii. 28.

His character, His life, His every action are stamped with the impress of unity. The claim that He acts at one moment on the divine level as God, and at another on the human level as man, is entirely to misinterpret the Gospel record. There is no division in His Person, no hint of conflicting and diverse elements. There is a simplicity, a directness, a unity of action, aim and purpose which preclude the thought of a divided personality. In Him may be recognised " perfect humanity on the level of deity," [31] and just as for Him there are not two worlds, the seen and the unseen, but one, and that God's, so He is God and man, yet not two Christs, but One.

[31] Thornton, *op. cit.*, p. 248.

SYNOPSIS.

A BROAD view of human nature and life reveals on the one hand its worth, and on the other its failure and non-attainment on its own level. They need to be taken up to a higher level than the natural, on which they may, by transformation, attain their full range and perfection. It was the recognition of these truths which largely guided the Church in its formulation of the doctrine of Christ. It was guided rather by the demands of human need and experience than by those of metaphysical speculation. Yet the Incarnation, if it is central to human life, must be central also for human thought. Both S. Paul and S. John recognised this fact, and related the Incarnation to the whole created order. It was seen to be the final term of God's relation to the world, as given in the record of the Old Testament. The organic view of the world, in which modern thought is finding increasing satisfaction, represents a conception of reality which in a high degree both illustrates and is illustrated by the Incarnation. It pictures the world as built up of successive levels of existence, each taken up and in turn transformed by a transcending principle of unity, which gives worth and significance to the level reached and to those below it. Highest in the organic series stands man, reaching out to the eternal order, yet unable to attain it by his own capacity for self-transcendence. Hence the necessity of a gracious movement from above and beyond, by which the eternal order is incorporated into the time series on the level of man in a final and absolute form and re-fashions it into its own likeness. The Incarnation is the coming to full self-manifestation of the immanent idea as present and potent in the whole creative process of the world conceived of in its organic aspect.

III. THE INCARNATION AND THE CREATED ORDER.

In the preceding lecture the truth of the Incarnation was approached primarily from the standpoint of human experience. It was viewed as the safeguard and sanction of certain ultimate human values and the satisfaction of certain ultimate human needs. It was also shown that it was in fact this standpoint which, whether in apostolic or later periods, largely governed its dogmatic formulation. Primary among those experiences, which Christ was found to mediate and convey, were those of revelation and redemption. In Him man's age-long quest for the knowledge of God was met and satisfied, and the Word spoken which was recognised as final in its declaration of God. Moreover, this revelation of God was discerned not so much in Christ's message about God as in Christ Himself. In Christ men saw revealed the truth of God in terms of human nature and human life. Yet human need runs deeper than that of knowledge and revelation. He needs a power, not his own, to deliver him from himself, to lift him above himself, to set him free from the bondage of his lower nature. And this power of redemptive grace was also found in Christ. In the experience of the believer Christ was proved to be his Deliverer, emancipating him from the moral fetters which he was impotent in his own strength to sever, and re-creating him on His own level.

Nor was it only the individual experience of revelation and redemption of which Christ was found in experience to be the source and sanction. In Him was also found the ground and basis of a new and higher social order. To Him, as its living background, was seen to run back the corporate life of the Christian community, with its intimate experience of a mutual love and fellowship which lifted human relationships to a supernatural level. Such were among those new and rich experiences mediated by Christ which were kept prominently in view in the gradual formulation of the doctrine of His Person.

The same standpoint of human experience in its bearing on the truth of Christ's Person may be presented on larger lines. On a broad view of human life two facts emerge into clear prominence, on the one hand the pervading sense of the worth of human nature and human life, on the other hand an equally pervading sense of its failure and non-attainment so long as it is confined within its own limits. Its insistent claim is that it should not be destroyed: yet equally insistent is its need of being fulfilled on a higher level than its own. Its primary claim is that its inherent worth should be recognised: and no scheme of salvation which involves the suppression or supersession of human nature and life can hope to win the unconditioned allegiance of mankind. When any such attempts to cramp and limit human nature or character, or the natural range of human interest and enterprise, have been made, they have led again and again to an insurgent recoil of

emancipation, and to the assertion of an irresistible claim to the recognition of the
inalienable rights of human life. Often indeed
the achievement of a truer and fuller manifestation of the Christian spirit and character
has been reached by a spontaneous pagan
movement of recoil against an iron-cast discipline
exerted in the supposed interests of religion itself.
Ethical qualities which mark the natural man and
elicit his admiration have their own worth, and
demand recognition as something far other and
more than " splendid vices." Similarly in the field
of enquiry and knowledge, the sphere of creative
art, the broad domain of industrial and commercial
enterprise, the realm of marriage and love, and the
large field of physical prowess, the factor of inherent
value, indeed of ultimate worth, is there claiming a
right appreciation and denied only with fatal results.
The great spheres of human achievement in the
ancient world, of law and administration in the
Roman, of speculation and art in the Hellenic, of
religious experience and aspiration in the East, these
proved themselves to have an inherent worth and
dignity which no higher demands could rightly or
safely repudiate or deny. Thus human nature and
life, and its spontaneous expressions, individual or
corporate, must find scope and freedom in any
economy or order complete and satisfying to
humanity.

Yet with all this there is another side. The full
recognition of the worth of human nature and of the
creative activities of man needs balancing with the

correlative truth of the insufficiency and imperfection of human character and achievement in itself. With all his achievements, and indeed the higher his achievements in the ethical and creative spheres, there is a sense of an unreached beyond which eludes man's utmost endeavour. In himself and in his work there is an unfinished character which demands fulfilment by subservience to a higher law. Attempts to build the complete fabric of human life from below have failed : nor can the full story of man's life be summed up in any process of evolution which rules out the entrance of new factors and forces and is regarded as a steady onward growth from below and within towards complete freedom and maturity. Across the whole page of the human record so looked at, there is written the fact of non-attainment. In himself and in his own proper nature man belongs to the ephemeral order which is doomed to pass away. From dust he comes, and to dust he must return. In the sphere of character his aspirations after goodness, the higher they are, the more they are seen to be incapable of full fruition within the limits of his own moral endeavour. His greatest achievements in the sphere of creative activity and skill are not only themselves subject to the forces of destruction, but point to " another country " which man aspires after yet in his own strength cannot reach. Hence with all their dignity and worth, and the full recognition so claimed, human character and life yet call for fulfilment by submission to a higher law than any which belongs to them on their own level. They call for a " dayspring from on high " to visit them,

with redemptive recreative powers. For their perfection and the attainment of their highest law of
being, they need to be taken up into an eternal order,
transcendent and above the temporal order to which
they belong, in which they may be lost to be found
again on the level of their full range and perfection.
Nor if full satisfaction is to be attained, can any
element of human nature, or any sphere of human
activity, remain outside the influence of this redemptive recreative power. Any such domain of
human life, which asserts its self-sufficiency and
repudiates submission to a higher law, is self-
condemned to the region of failure and non-attainment, carries within itself the seeds of degeneration
and retrogression, and by its self-chosen refusal of
the call to " pass over " from the old order to the
new, to which the other spheres have yielded, must
vitiate the whole movement of redemption. For
human life is one, and no element can stand outside
the regenerative process of fulfilment on a higher
level without thwarting and holding back the full
reach and range of the remainder.

It is this twofold experience of human life, of
worth and imperfection, of the claim to full recognition yet of the need of redemption, for which room
must be found in any satisfying doctrine of the
Person of Christ. It was indeed this very demand,
as we have seen, which guided the Church in reject-
ing or accepting formulations of this doctrine put
forward for its consideration. It was clearly
recognised that in any such formulation as it could
accept room must be found for these truths and

needs of human life. They form essential data to the doctrine of His Person : and no such doctrine could prove acceptable to the Church, however far it appealed to the speculative mind, if it ruled out any element which entered as an essential factor into these values and experiences. Hence the Church was largely guided not by the dictates of metaphysical speculation but by those of human need and experience in formulating its doctrine of Christ. It ruled out, as heretical, various definitions put forward rather in the interests of logical consistency than of religious value : and we have seen that the formula in which at the close of the long-drawn Christological controversy it finally expressed its own belief on the subject was mainly valuable as authoritatively safeguarding those elements of Christ's Person which had been found essential to Christian experience, and of which, therefore, account must be taken in any satisfying formulation of the doctrine of His Person, rather than as providing a definition ultimately satisfying to human thought. Indeed, it may well be that no such formulation was possible within the categories of ancient thought. For, as we have seen, axiomatic to ancient thought and to the terms in which it found expression, was an inherent dualism between Godhead and manhood, the Godhead being invested with a changeless impassibility which by its very nature cannot become the subject of finite and temporal experience, and manhood being thought of, in contrast with Godhead, as in itself mortal, changeable and sinful. Regarded as such, there could be no union between the two. So long as Godhead and

manhood were held rigidly apart as mutually inconsistent it was impracticable to view them each in its
perfection as united in the Person of Christ. The
truth of the Incarnation could only be accepted at
the cost of surrendering the axiomatic assumptions
of current thought, and consistency could only be
purchased at the cost of surrendering one element or
the other in the unity of Christ's Person. Yet this
was a solution which the Church could not accept,
concerned as it was in its formularies to safeguard,
at whatever cost to the claims of abstract thought,
those truths and values which were the background
of its own religious life and experience. Indeed it
was only by subordinating the demands of metaphysical speculation to those of religious experience,
that, in its credal or conciliar formulations on the
subject, the Church safeguarded the truth of the
Incarnation.

Yet it cannot be satisfactory to leave the Incarnation as an isolated phenomenon unrelated to, and
indeed inconsistent with, men's conception of the
universe as a whole. It is not enough, as indeed
was early recognised, to make human need and
experience the only test of its truth. If it was true,
it must be true not only in its practical response to
human need, but true for reality as a whole. It
must be integrated into men's conception of the
whole order of reality. If it was, as had been proved,
so central to human experience and need, it must be
central also to the conception and constitution of the
world as a whole. The truth of the Incarnation
must be seen not only to constitute the sanction and

source of a unique human experience, but to be of central significance for man's conception of the whole created order.   Moreover, those conceptions of the universe in which human thought found, or should find, an increasing measure of rest and satisfaction, must themselves illuminate and be illuminated by the truth of Christ's Person, if the latter was to occupy that central place which religious experience assigned to it.   Hence the necessity of seeking and finding an explanation of the Person of Christ satisfying to human thought as well as adequate to human life.   In the last resort the claims of metaphysical coherence must be satisfied as well as those of religious need.   Such an explanation can only be reached by viewing the fact of Christ against the background of the universe or created order as a whole.   It was indeed in this direction that already within the apostolic period such an explanation was looked for.   Already S. Paul represents the Person of Christ as integral to the whole created order, the origin, channel and governing principle of all things that are. "In Him were all things created . . all things hath been created through Him, and unto Him; and He is before all things, and in Him all things consist." [1]   Thus S. Paul passes behind the Incarnation, and the Christ who is the Head of the Church, to the pre-existent Christ and Head of the created order ; and the " Eternal Word is seen as holding the same relation to the Universe, which the Incarnate Christ holds to the Church.   He is the source of its life, the centre of all its developments, the

[1] Col. i. 16f.

mainspring of all its motives," [2] " the channel and the goal of Creation." [3]

So, too, the prologue of S. John represents a similar recognition of the need of viewing the Incarnation not as an isolated unrelated phenomenon but in its intimate connection with the world order. Under the title of the Logos, Christ is viewed on the one hand as belonging to the transcendent and eternal order, and on the other as the immanent idea and creative agent of the whole world-series, its light, its life and its principle of creative energy : and the Incarnation is the " Word made Flesh," the actual-isation in the Person of Jesus Christ of that immanent word or thought which was present and potent throughout as the governing and guiding principle of the whole order of creation. For both S. Paul and S. John it is probable that the sources from which they derived their conception of the cosmic significance of Christ were the Hebrew Scriptures rather than current Greek speculation. It is in the Old Testament that, as we have already seen, there is to be found the historical background of the Incarnation, and, in terms of a concrete historical record, the affirmation of that relation between God and the created order, including man, which is pre-supposed in the Incarnation. And it was by a con-stant return to that scriptural record, enshrining the spiritual experience of a people, that the Church and its thinkers were safeguarded from formulations of doctrine, derived from the categories of Greek

[2] Lightfoot : *Epistles to the Colossians and Philemon*, p. 216.
[3] Radford : *Epistles to the Colossians and Philemon*, p. 176.

speculation, which would have failed to do justice to the fact of the Incarnation and to its religious values. " What emerges from the evidence is that the revelation of God given in Holy Scripture was regarded as governing and controlling the development of men's thoughts about the Christ." [4]   And it is to these same Holy Scriptures and their historical record of God's revealed relation to man and the created order that again and again we must revert to test and prove such formulations of the doctrine of Christ in modern times as we may be led to attempt.

The problem of Christ then cannot be divorced from the problem of God, and of God's relation to the created order, indeed of the creative process itself.   The Incarnation can only be rightly viewed as the final term and expression of the revealed relation between the divine and the human, between God and the created order, of which the Old Testament is the classical historical record.   And in the terms of that record of religious experience, as interpreted by the seers and prophets of Israel, God the transcendent and infinite One is yet also the guiding immanent principle of the creative process and of human history.   He does not stand aloof as the unconditioned and unconditionable.   Creation itself involves, indeed consists in, a divine self-limitation, under which God the Infinite and Eternal brings Himself within, conditions Himself by, the temporal finite series.   And the Incarnation is thus the revelation in final and absolute form of what God has revealed Himself to be throughout in relation to

[4] Thornton, *op. cit.,* p. 8.

the created order and to humanity. Thus the doctrine of the Incarnation must both stand the test and
itself be the test of human thought on the ultimate
problem of the relation of eternity to time, of the
eternal to the temporo-spatial series : and the more
true to reality as a whole and so ultimately acceptable such solution of this ultimate problem as is
offered proves to be, the more will that solution
throw light upon and itself be illuminated by the
truth of the Incarnation. Now it is the organic view
of the world in which modern thought is finding its
most secure and satisfying resting place : and we
believe that in terms of that standpoint can be presented a conception of the Incarnation which, while
including and safeguarding those religious values
which in experience have been derived from it, is
also adequate to the claims of human thought and
of a self-consistent view of the world as a whole.

[5] The view in question represents or pictures the
world as built up of successive levels of creaturely
existence, in which the lower level in each case only
attains its full expression and significance as it is
taken up to a higher level, and in the process is not
destroyed or eliminated but renewed and transformed. At each level there is a " transcending
principle of unity " which gives character and meaning to the order of existence represented by that level,
and to those lower strata which by transformation
are themselves included in that order. Such is the
organic series, in which each level " is taken up by

[5] The section which follows is an attempt to summarise the
main argument of Thornton's *Incarnate Lord*.

transformation to conform to an ascending process, in which the determining factors are principles of unity transcending succession." [6] Each stage in the series reaches a relative completion through the transcending principle of unity proper to it. " At every stage in the ascending series of the universe there is an entry of creative activity and an emergence of new factors and conditions which are the products of that activity." [7] Yet each stage is incomplete in relation to the series as a whole, and indeed only gains its ultimate significance by reference to the whole and when it is itself taken up and transformed on higher levels. In other words, each stage points beyond itself to that by the presence of which it alone attains fulness of being, character and significance.

Moreover, the highest law of being proper to each level is not the product of that level and does not emerge from within it. It supervenes from above and from without. It is a " principle of transcendence " which is given from above and which itself confers being and character on that order of existence at which it supervenes and which it pervades. It is the manifestation proper to that level of an eternal order beyond and above the whole organic series and each level of it, yet the background of the whole and reaching down to each level of the series in the degree and manner possible to that level, to give it its rightful place and character in the whole series. The eternal order as so conceived is thus a principle of creative activity transcendent above yet

[6] *op. cit.,* p. 76.   [7] *op. cit.,* p. 44.

immanent in the organic series, refashioning each level of existence in a way which transforms but does not supersede or overwhelm it. And the advance from lower to higher levels in the organic series is determined by the degree in which the level reached includes, transforms and illuminates all other and lower levels of existence, while yet itself pointing to a beyond which it must attain if in its turn its value and significance for the whole is to be revealed. So through the successive levels of the created order the organic series is constituted, the higher level in each case, through the transcending principle of unity proper to it, giving value and meaning to all that precedes, and advancing in significance as it becomes increasingly capable of embodying and embracing within itself a higher measure of that eternal order which is both other than and beyond the series and at the same time is incorporated within it in ever greater measure.

To the organic series as so constituted man belongs. As integrated into that series he is indeed its last term, its crowning point. In him the whole series culminates and every stage in it finds its true place and meaning. " The significance of the series as a whole is clearly to be looked for at its upper end, where the eternal order becomes dominant " [8] : and man represents that upper end, precisely because he has and knows himself to have an affinity with that eternal order unshared by the lower stages of the series. He is constituted " on the level of spirit." " There is in man the principle of self-transcendence

[8] *op. cit.,* p. 75.

by which he has contact with the eternal order." [9]
He is conscious of the categorical claims of that
order, beyond and other than himself, upon him, and
that only by adequate response to those claims can
he obey the highest law of his being. Conformity
with the claims of that order constitutes for him that
transcending principle of unity, through which he,
and through him the whole organic series, can reach
his, and its, goal. A creature of two worlds, he is
rooted in the organic order of existence, yet knows
that his true home lies elsewhere : and his supreme
aim is by self-transcendence to span the gulf which
lies between him and the organic order of existence,
to which he belongs, and that other world which he
seeks to attain, yet which constantly eludes his attainment. For, try as he will, he cannot attain by his
own effort. His capacity for self-transcendence is
inherently inadequate to the need. Stand though
he does at its head, yet he " belongs to the cosmic
series, and is marked with the same limitations " [10]
and " shares its unfinished character." In religious
language man is " a creature who cannot span the
gulf which lies between himself and his Creator." [11]
Moreover, this consciousness of non-attainment is
most acute in the moral sphere. If truth lies ever
beyond him, yet more so does goodness. Indeed, the
further he progresses in the moral sphere, the more
distant does the goal seem to be   " The goal recedes
as we approach it and those who have advanced
furthest along that path are precisely those who are

[9] *op. cit.*, p. 116.   [11] *op. cit.*, p. 121.
[10] *op. cit.*, p. 113.

most conscious of non-attainment." [12]   Moreover,
the failure of man to rise above himself, to apprehend and fully respond to the claims of the eternal
order, is reflected backwards over the whole creation
which, in its measure, shares that non-attainment,
that frustration of which man is conscious.

So the gulf between the organic series and the
eternal order remains unspanned, even in and by
man, the highest level of that series. For man is in
himself essentially incomplete, an unfinished organism, who cannot attain an autonomous harmony of
self-adjustment. Yet it is in and by man that the
final step must be taken. For the law of advance
throughout is not that of supersession but that of
transformation : and if the transcendent principle
of unity proper to man, and through man to the
whole series, were one which set aside or overrode
man's nature and distinctive gifts and qualities, the
character of the whole process would be vitiated at
its highest point. Hence for man the highest law
of his being, the creative activity which carries him
to attainment, must both supervene from without
yet find expression and embodiment on the human
level. " Our experience of the eternal order shows
that harmony can be effected only by a self-
transcendence which carries man utterly beyond
himself; and yet that same transcendence of self
must be effected by an activity which expresses the
whole self and which is therefore self-determining." [13]
For this purpose, the eternal order, which as we have
seen is other than and beyond the time series yet

---

[12] *op. cit.*, p. 119.   [13] *op. cit.*, p. 197.

immanent within it, must be incorporated in some final and absolute form into that series on the human level. Man at the head of the organic series cannot by his own capacity for self-transcendence attain his goal in the eternal order. If, then, that goal, the goal not only of humanity but of the whole organic series, is to be reached, the eternal order, by its principle of creative activity, must in a final and absolute form take up into itself and re-fashion into its own likeness man, and with man the whole temporal order embodied in him. Man must attain and can only attain his goal by a gracious movement from without and above of recreative and redemptive activity which, acting on the level of humanity and without overriding man's nature, enables him to effect that crowning act of self-transcendence of which by his own effort he is incapable.

And it is this which in religious terms is meant by the Incarnation. For the Incarnation is the incorporation of the eternal order into the organic and temporal series in a final and absolute form. In the Person of Jesus Christ, not humanity only, but the whole created order, to which humanity belongs and at the head of which it stands, is taken into God. In the Person of Jesus Christ, not humanity only, but the whole created order is subjected to that transcendent principle of unity which gives to the whole series and to every stage within it its ultimate significance. For in the Person of Jesus Christ the two worlds of the eternal order and the organic series find their point of ultimate union and reconciliation. He is perfect Man, and, as such, stands

within the organic series. He has all that is proper
to human nature. In Him no element of human
nature, no value of human life, no expression of the
human spirit is denied or superseded. Indeed, in
Him the whole created order, and not humanity only,
is revealed as of worth and significance. His Godhead in no way involves the supersession or forfeiture of that which belongs to humanity and to the
natural order. But He is also perfect God, and, as
such, not only does He stand on the other side and
belong to the eternal order, but the eternal order is
constituted in Him. Not only was He " with God " :
He was, and is, " Very God." Within the organic
series, He is yet not of it, nor does He emerge from
within it. He enters it from beyond : and it is this
very fact of His complete transcendence which gives
its ultimate significance to manhood and to the whole
temporal order to which, in the Incarnation, He
makes Himself subject. In Him Godhead is revealed
not as the unconditioned and unconditionable
Absolute, and as such by its very nature debarred
from entering into relationship with man and the
visible order. Godhead is revealed as indeed the
eternal and the transcendent, yet also and increasingly as entering into and incorporating into itself
the temporal series, as self-conditioned and self-
limited by entry into the finite tempero-spatial order
of existence.

Thus in the Person of Jesus Christ a conception
of God and of Godhead is involved and receives its
final sanction which is wholly remote from the
Deism of Gnostic speculation, and which views Him

F

as One who by His own creative will intervenes on the plane of human life, enters into the conditions of human nature and lifts it to the Divine level. And on its side manhood is revealed in its full range and perfection, as not in itself and by its very nature mortal, peccable and subject to change and corruption. Manhood is revealed, when at its truest and highest, as taken into God, receiving the impress of Deity, and as lifted into that region where what is " mortal has put on immortality " and there is no sin or death. For be it remembered that the true stature and standard of humanity must not be looked for as it is in us, and apart from Him, brought under the dominion of imperfection and failure, of sin and death. It is to be sought and found as it is in Him, united with God, self-transcended by union with the Divine, and in us in so far as through Him we share His union with God. Thus that conception of Godhead on the one hand and of Manhood on the other which is presupposed in the Incarnation, of which indeed the Incarnation is the ultimate corroboration, finds vindication in that organic theory of the world which is characteristic of modern thought. Nor need the fact of Christ be regarded as an isolated phenomenon of history which can only be accepted at the cost of turning our backs on all that we have learned or come to think of humanity and the world as a whole. It is the final word of that organic order which is constituted by the increasing entry of the eternal into the time series, as the latter is carried to ever higher levels, and which demands at its highest point, that of manhood constituted on the level of spirit, the incorporation of that transcendent and eternal order in a final and absolute form for its full significance and the attainment of its highest law of being.

From the more immanental standpoint again it may be well to attempt to state the truth of the Incarnation in relation to the organic conception of the universe already outlined. For that organic conception presupposes throughout the presence and control of an immanent idea or principle governing and informing the whole creative process. An organism is constituted by " an ideal principle," [14] the " idea of the good of the whole," [15] which constitutes its life, defines its character, and assigns it its place in the whole order of reality. It is in the presence and potency of the idea of the whole that is to be found the character of the organism, the law of its growth, the standard of its perfection. Such an idea is partially and obscurely expressed in the lower and earlier stages of its advance, and reaches full and concrete manifestation with the development of the organism to its natural maturity.

It is this conception of the immanent principle or idea of the whole, as informing and fashioning the organism, which may rightly be applied not merely to particular organisms, but to the world as a whole. In so far at least as the world can be viewed in an organic aspect, it too presupposes the presence and energy of a governing idea or principle as giving

[14] *The Spirit and the Incarnation:* Walker, p. 261.
[15] *op. cit.,* p. 261.

order, form and direction to the whole process of development : and " the history of the world must be," in accordance with this conception, " the growing manifestation of this divine principle of its life, which is . . . the increasing entrance of the divine life into finite forms of manifestation, till at length it appears in the fulness of the original Divine Thought." [16] So conceived, the Incarnation represents the embodiment in final and complete form of that which throughout had been the immanent idea of the whole, present throughout and increasingly evidenced in the world's life, the " Divine Thought of the Creation fully expressing itself." [17]

This conception of the Incarnation has a close affinity with that which governs the prologue of S. John. For the Logos of the passage in question is precisely the ruling idea of the whole or thought of God, viewed as the governing principle of the creative process, which " was in the world," [18] striving to realise and express itself, as forms and moulds of self-expression were available, and at last " made flesh " [19] in the Person of Jesus Christ. Thus " in the beginning " [20] and throughout " God was in Christ " [21] as the idea and principle of the whole created order. From the beginning and throughout there was a Divine outgoing and self-limitation, a conditioning of the unconditioned, a self-emptying on the part of God that He might realise Himself in and through the created order. From the beginning

[16] op. cit., p. 262.
[17] op. cit., p. 257.
[18] Jn. i. 10.
[19] Jn. i. 14.
[20] Jn. i. 1.
[21] 2 Cor. v. 19.

and throughout, that Word or idea, the idea of the whole, was seeking a perfect organ of expression, through which God could be manifested in the world not as impersonal idea or potency, but as and in Himself through a " body prepared for " [22] Him. The mystery of the Incarnation is also the mystery of creation.   The latter, too, involves and is constituted by a divine self-emptying or limitation, and " the world is thus founded in an act of divine self-sacrifice." [23]

It is then in Christ and in the " holy fellowship," the new humanity, of which Christ is the Head, that the idea of the whole organic order is at length realised and manifested in its fulness and perfection. Till His coming into the world as Man, that Word or immanent principle was present as idea and potency only, working in impersonal form, yet ever seeking and finding less and less inadequate forms of self-expression.   Moreover, that Word or idea of the whole was not only " with God " [24] : it " was God " [24] : and it is God as Son, God as eternally offering within the Godhead the response of Sonship to the Father's will, who is the Divine idea or principle of the whole, immanent throughout the creative process, stamping upon it its true character, governing its development, ordering its consummation.   Ever God as Son was seeking to clothe Himself with more adequate forms of self-manifestation, to come to and realise Himself in and through nature and the created order, so that " the entire idea of

---

[22] Heb. x. 5.   Cp. Ps. xl. 6.   [24] Jn. i. 1.
[23] Walker, *op. cit.,* p. 307.

Divine Sonship, which lies as potentiality behind the whole, shall be expressed in the consummation." [25]

Now it is in man and on the human level that alone and at last the idea or immanent principle governing the whole creative process could realise its final and perfect consummation.   For man is differentiated from the created order as a whole, of which he yet forms a part, as possessing a capacity for sonship, for filial response and outgoing love to God, which we have seen is the very idea of the world's life, the very nature of God as He is present within the created order and gives it value and significance.   It is this capacity for sonship which forms the point of union between man and God. Yet the humanity which could be the vehicle of the Word, of God as Son, is not humanity in itself, or in its lower and more primitive form, still less as marred and tainted by sin.   It is humanity on the level of spirit, as rendered by the Holy Spirit capable of full and adequate response, as realising in fulness its potentiality for sonship, through humanity as such, that the Divine could manifest itself within it, and the Son of God, or God as Son, enter the world. Thus in the Incarnation God as Son is self-realised and self-manifested in human form.   " It is God as Son, as He has gone out from Himself, to become the principle and ideal of the world's life, realising His life in the fulness of time in that human form which He was seeking, and as the result of all the working of God as Word and Spirit in nature and in man." [26]

[25] Walker, *op. cit.,* p. 306.   [26] Walker, *op. cit.,* p. 281.

On the one hand then, the Incarnation is a new creation. It is not the mere emergence by an inevitable process of evolution of that which was already present. It was from above and beyond, a real entry of God into the created order on the level of humanity. Yet it was also the coming to conscious self-expression and to concrete and personal embodiment of that which had been present throughout as the idea of the whole, the outcome and issue of the whole creative process, a process in which the Divine had throughout been preparing for Himself less imperfect forms of self-expression, present at its lowest levels from inanimate to animate, from animate to conscious, and ever seeking a perfect organ of self-manifestation. Thus while something wholly new and unique, the Incarnation was yet " conditioned by the previous preparatory working of the one Divine Spirit, and was the result of the continuous working of that Spirit " [27]; and the Christ stands as God self-manifested as Man, as Man found capable of expressing God. In Christ and in the new order of redeemed humanity of which Christ is the Head, the divine principle of the whole organic order of the world comes to conscious and final self-expression, gives the whole creative process its significance, and is the end and consummation of that which was " in the beginning."

[27] Walker, *op. cit.,* p. 335.

SYNOPSIS.

THE Church's task throughout has been both to safeguard and to apply the truth of the Incarnation, as final and regulative in the spheres of thought and of life. With a denial of the Incarnation, as S. John saw, goes a life which is other and less than Christian. Gnosticism with its dualistic teaching as to the relations of God and the world, the soul and the body, was such a denial, issuing in a non-Christian moral standard of extreme asceticism or of unrestrained licentiousness. Manichæism, Paulicianism, and the Albigensian heresy represent later phases of a similar dualism, and a denial of the full implications of the truth of the Incarnation. So with Puritanism and much modern Protestantism. Christian Science, with its exclusive stress on the spiritual, is a modern form of Gnosticism The Church as not only the guardian but the embodiment of the truth of the Incarnation, is called to bring under law to Christ all mankind and all realms of human activity. Such was the task and such largely the achievement of the early and mediæval Church. Indeed the excessive dominance of purely religious interests over the whole of human life in the Middle Ages led to a recoil of emancipation at the Renaissance : and the modern era is characterised by a growing secularisation in all spheres of human activity public and private. The present task of the Church is to redress the balance, and to reassert the principles of the Incarnation throughout the whole order of modern civilisation.

IV. THE INCARNATION AND THE MISSION OF THE CHURCH.

WE have traced in the briefest outline the process by which the Church was led to safeguard and define the truth of the Incarnation : and we have seen that its principal service during the period of the Christological controversies and Councils was to preserve those factors, for which, however apparently inconsistent with each other, room must be found in any doctrine of the Person of Christ claiming general recognition. The perfect Godhead and perfect Manhood of Christ, together with the unity of His Person, these were the truths which, at whatever cost to logical consistency, must be presupposed and included in any satisfying doctrine or definition of the Incarnation. Attempts were made, as we have seen, to secure a logically consistent doctrine of the Person of Christ at the cost of the practical surrender of one or other of the truths for which both religious experience and the gospel portrait of Jesus stood : and the Church rejected these in turn, because they omitted from their reckoning one or other of those elements in the Person of Christ which must be preserved as the basis of those values which in religious experience are found to be mediated by Christ. And those values were preserved, even at the cost of failure at the time to reach a doctrine of the Person of Christ wholly satisfying to human thought. That failure was largely due to the presuppositions as to the nature of Godhead and manhood assumed as axiomatic in ancient thought : and we have found that the organic conception of the world towards which present day thought is feeling its way enables us to arrive at a statement or view of the Incarnation which, while inclusive of its essential factors, is also more adequate to the demands of philosophical enquiry.

We have now to consider those ultimate values and potentialities of human life, of which the truth of the Incarnation is the sanction and justification. From the apostolic age onwards, as has been seen, it was the demands of religious experience, and in particular the experiences of revelation and redemption as found in Christ, which were primary and determinant factors in the formulation of Christological doctrine. The truth of the Incarnation was recognised as ultimate and regulative in the spheres both of thought and of life, and therefore as one at any cost to be preserved. It is indeed this recognition which underlies the fierce insistence of the first epistle of S. John on the true humanity of Christ, indeed on the full truth of the Incarnation.

" Who is the liar but he that denieth that Jesus is the Christ? This is the antichrist, even he that denieth the Father and the Son." (1 Jn. ii. 22.)

" Hereby know ye the Spirit of God : every spirit which confesseth that Jesus Christ is come in the flesh is of God : and every spirit which confesseth not Jesus is not of God : and this is the spirit of the antichrist, whereof ye have heard that it cometh; and now it is in the world already." (1 Jn. iv. 2f.)

The writer sees the antichrist, the embodiment of all that was most inimical to Christianity and the Church, in the false prophet whose teaching involves a denial of the Incarnation. He is probably thinking in the immediate context of that form of Docetism or Adoptionism identified with the name of Cerinthus, which represented the Divine Christ as descending on the man Jesus at His baptism, and as leaving Him and " flying heavenwards " at His passion, which would not concede that in Jesus Christ God was made man, and that the Godhead and manhood were for ever united.

Here indeed, in the denial of the Incarnation, is the arch-heresy, appearing and reappearing, disguised under various names, and espoused by a succession of religious groups, right down the centuries of Christian history. It is the arch-heresy, because error here is of fatal consequence not only in the sphere of truth but in that of life, because to believe and to propagate heresy here is to be entangled and to entangle others in the bondage of that dualism, that clear-cut breach between God and man, the body and the soul, the spiritual and the material, from which the Incarnation and belief in the Incarnation is the only way of deliverance. S.John knows, as the Church has always instinctively known, that literally everything stands or falls with the truth of the Incarnation in the sphere of life as in that of thought. For once allow that in Jesus Christ the manhood was not taken into God, and you have a theory, a theology, on which a life can be consistently built up which is less than Christian, which carries with it an ethical standard which, whatever form it takes, cannot claim the sanction of Christ. For that ethical standard is grounded in the truth of the Incarnation, and the implication, involved in that truth, of the redemption and sanctification of the material through contact with the spiritual. It is they, whose religion is grounded in that truth, who in a peculiar sense have learned that most difficult of all arts, the art of living, of using without abusing the world, of being in the world yet not of it, of combining enjoyment of outward things with ascetic abstinence, of making right distinctions between what may be taken and what may be left, of reconciling world acceptance with world renunciation. On the other hand, the religion of those who have surrendered or ignored the truth of the Incarnation, as held and defined by the Church, has found its logical outcome in a reaction from the sacramental implications of the truth, in a theory and way of life which separates God from the world, which draws a hard and fast line between the sacred and the secular, which does not look for the spiritual in and through the outward, but over against it and in contrast with it, and which therefore fails to " discern the things which differ " in moral issues social and individual.

It is then the truth of the Incarnation, of Godhead and manhood united in the Person of Christ, which is not only the final revelation of God in relation to nature and man, but is the ground and basis of human life as lived at its truest and best. And conversely it is the denial, express or implicit, of one factor or of the other, and of the union of the two in the Person of Christ, which is the presupposition of alien and non-Christian conceptions of life and the social order. It is here indeed that is to be found that " heresy of the Orient," [1] which invaded and almost destroyed the Church in its earliest contacts with pagan philosophy and pagan life. Under the term Gnosticism may be summed up a conglomerate of fantastic speculations propagated by different teachers on matters concerning the world, man and Deity. " Among the ferment of conflicting religions, cults and systems which fought for recognition in the Orient, Gnosticism in its manifold and tangled varieties may be used as a convenient label for grouping together schools of thought which, in more or less distant touch with Christianity, sought access to the Divine through other modes, mythological, ceremonial, mystic or speculative than those of self-revelation to a chosen people, or incarnation in a divine Son." [2] This, at least, however the various forms of Gnosticism had in common, that they postulated a radical dualism between spirit and the visible tangible order of nature. The creation of the latter they attributed to a deity lower than and different from the supreme God, a being ineffable and remote, debarred by His very nature from any form of conditioning relation with the material world. They thus assumed as axiomatic the impossibility of contact between God on the one hand and human flesh and the material world on the other.

[1] See *Church Times*, p. 707, June, 1931.
[2] *Epistle of S. James and Judaic Christianity;* Randall, p. 119.

This dualism between God and the world of nature was reflected in a corresponding cleavage between the soul and body of man. The body was regarded as the unclean and evil tenement of the soul, its destiny not to be redeemed but destroyed, while the welfare of the soul consisted in release from its fleshly prison. But they went further than theory in the separation which they made between body and soul. They carried the theory logically into its moral consequences. Indeed for practical purposes Gnostics may be divided into "the ascetic and licentious sects: both parties agreeing in holding the essential evil of matter: the one endeavouring by rigorous abstinence to free as much as possible man's soul from the bondage to which it is subjected by union with his material part . . . . . the other abandoning as desperate any attempt to purify the hopelessly corrupt body, and teaching that the instructed soul ought to hold itself unaffected by the deeds of the body." [3]

Here then was Gnosticism in theory and practice. It did not represent an honest attempt to formulate a doctrine of the Person of Christ on the basis of the gospels and of Christian experience. It derived from further back, and brought with it as its root assumption a doctrine of God and of humanity which excluded the possibility of an Incarnation. That doctrine was not derived from the Old Testament and from the tradition of belief which is characteristic of Hebrew religion. In the Jewish conception of God, and of God's relation to man, the Incarna-

[3] Murray's *Dictionary of Christian Biography,* p. 395.

tion, as we have seen, found its natural historical background. Gnostic belief, on the other hand, was drawn from oriental sources, unaffected by the revealed religion of Israel. It left unbridged and unbridgeable the gulf between man and God. It condemned as inherently evil the human body and the physical world of which the human body formed a part. By implication, if not by open avowal, it was a denial of Jesus Christ " come in the flesh " : and it found practical expression in a standard of life, which whether on the ascetic or the licentious side, was poles asunder from the standard presupposed by the Incarnation.

With no little strain and difficulty the Church discharged from its system the poison of Gnostic heresy : and Gnosticism as such ceased to afflict it. But in certain respects at least it took fresh shape under other names at recurring epochs through the succeeding centuries, and has its counterparts in the present day. Its essential dualism, as between God and the world, so between the soul and body of man, reappeared in Manichæism, emerging in the third century from Babylonia, and possessing marked affinities both with Zoroastrism and Buddhism. As a philosophy it was " based upon the idea of the essential and eternal contrast between good and evil, between light and darkness." [4] But it carried these forms of legitimate dualism into other and unwarranted regions. For it, too, the body was not the expression and vehicle but the prison of the spirit of

[4] Hastings' *Encyclopædia of Religion and Ethics,* Vol. VIII., p. 397.

man.   Hence the inevitable inference that the divine element in man must be emancipated from its fetters in order that it may return to its heavenly source. The moral outcome of its teaching was the need of crushing the body by ascetic discipline as the necessary method of emancipating the soul.   It adopted characteristically a Docetic view of the Incarnation : for if the body was the creation of an evil principle and the prison of the soul, it could not be the habitation of the Christ.   " Moreover, the Son, when He came for man's salvation, assumed a human appearance, so that He appeared to men as if He were a man, and men thought that He had been born." [5] Thus it was based on the separation of those " natures " found united in the Incarnation, and it carried with it the assumption that the body was not for the Lord but for destruction.   It was the parent of those systems of ultra-Puritan outlook and life, which put asunder what God has joined together. From the East it spread westwards to find congenial soil in Egypt and North Africa, where, as illustrated pre-eminently in S. Augustine, himself for a time captured by Manichæan logic, the dark and gloomy, divisive and twice-born type of religious experience was indigenous to the people and the land.   It is true that Augustine became the leading champion of Catholic orthodoxy against Manichæan heresy, yet it is doubtful whether he ever entirely threw off those dualistic presuppositions which underlay Manichæan teaching.   There are and remain at least elements in

[5] Epiph. Haer. lxvi. 49 (quoted Murray's *Dictionary of Christian Biography,* p. 684).

his teaching which isolated from the rest can be interpreted, as indeed they have been, in Calvinistic Puritan circles in a sharply dualistic sense.

Later in date, but also originating in Asia, and equally dualistic in doctrine and morals, were the Paulicians. Making their appearance under that name, whether, as Gibbon says, from a " devotion to the writings and character of S. Paul," [6] or for some other reason, in the seventh century, they played a not unimportant part in the political and religious life of the Eastern Empire. Gibbon speaks of them as " a branch of Manichæans," who, " presumed to reconcile the doctrines of Zoroaster and Christ " : and whether or not they derived their teaching directly from Manichæan sources they were characterised by a similar dualistic conception of the government of the world, and an Adoptionist doctrine of the Person of Christ. The Christ only took possession of the Man, Jesus, at His Baptism. " It was then He became Chief of beings, heavenly and earthly, then He became the Light of the World . . . then He was filled with the Godhead." [7]

Paulicianism was a Puritan recoil from Catholic teaching and practice. It rejected the priesthood, denied the real presence of Christ " either on the Cross or in the Eucharist," [8] and made its appeal to the letter of Scripture. It carried with it, like Manichæanism, a dualistic conception of the relation of spirit and body, and issued in an ascetic standard

[6] *Decline and Fall,* ch. liv.
[7] *Key of Truth:* ed. Conybeare, p. 75. (Quoted : *Dictionary of Religion and Ethics,* ix. 696.)
[8] Gibbon : *op. cit.*

G

of morality and in the practice of abstinence from contact with the material, particularly in marriage and procreation, as " involving a certain defilement." The Paulicians gained a strong footing in Asia Minor and Armenia. They were persecuted from time to time by orthodox emperors and revenged themselves upon them in alliance with the Saracens. In the eighth century a numerous colony of them was planted in Constantinople and Thrace, and settled at Philippopolis. Thence they spread westwards through Italy to France, where their teaching later took root among the Albigenses of Languedoc.

For in all probability the Albigensian heresy had at least in part a Paulician origin. The teaching of the Cathari, as they were called in the earlier stages of the heresy, was equally marked by a " Gnostic-dualistic tendency." The heresy as it took shape in the South of France derived its title from the Albigeois of Languedoc, the name being first given to it in the early years of the thirteenth century, when the censure of Innocent III. fell heavily upon it, and a concerted and successful attempt was made through the persuasive preaching of the Dominicans, backed by the Inquisition and the sword of Simon de Montfort, to eradicate it and all who professed it. No justification can be found for the bloody persecution to which the Albigenses were subjected. None the less, the dualistic heresy which they professed was not only subversive of Catholic truth but fatal to Christian life.[9]

[9] See *Dictionary of Religion and Ethics,* I. p. 281. " The doctrine of the Cathari had assumed a form which can only be described as subversive not only of the teaching of the Western Church, but of Christianity itself."

This same strain of Gnostic dualism, and of recoil from the full implications of the doctrine of the Incarnation, was a marked feature of the Puritan movement of the Reformation epoch. For if the Puritan movement gave a new sanction and dignity to secular work and business and thus redressed the balance of an excessive emphasis on the life of the cloister, it also cut off and repudiated as belonging to the domain of the devil whole fields of human activity, particularly in art, music and drama, recognised as legitimate expressions of the human spirit. It imposed on those who lived within the scope of its authority a tyrannical system of restrictive morality, a morality of taboos and prohibitions, based on arbitrary distinctions of right and wrong and enforced by public action. It was thus based on a non-sacramental view of human life and of nature, which drew a rigid line between the sacred and the secular. Thus it, too, was in principle a denial of the Incarnation in so far as the latter is the supreme example and the divine sanction of the claim " that both the secular and the spiritual have their imprescriptible rights," [10] and that "it is not by suppression that the spirit wins its victories, but by its power to transmute and transcend." [10]

It is, too, this Puritan dualistic strain, with its tendency to draw a false and arbitrary line between the sacred and the secular, which colours much modern Protestantism. For it, too, hesitates or refuses to claim the whole domain of human life

[10] *Cross-currents in English Literature of the Seventeenth Century:* (Grierson), p. 340.

for God. It tends to separate off certain expressions of the human spirit, certain spheres of human interest as beyond redemption, as outside the sphere of religion. It is largely non-sacramental in its outlook on the world and in its worship. It looks askance at the outward as an aid and vehicle of the inward in religious observance, and it characteristically relegates the sacraments themselves to a comparatively minor place in the ordinances of religion. So, too, its moral standard is largely restrictive and prohibitory, and, where it predominates in its extremer forms, it tends to develop into an arbitrary moral tyranny which inevitably provokes a violent recoil. That there is in the religion of the Incarnation a Puritan strain of renunciation and other-worldliness which from time to time needs special emphasis is abundantly true. The necessity of a stern and rigorous asceticism in the cultivation of the highest life is emphasised by our Lord and exemplified by S. Paul; and both history and Christian experience have abundantly vindicated the place of discipline, the negative road of ascetic mortification, of the renunciation of activities and interests in themselves legitimate and pure in the higher interests of the Kingdom of God. Yet there is all the difference in the world between an asceticism which cuts off the offending hand or plucks out the offending eye for the safeguarding and attainment of the highest end, and that which relegates to the realm of the devil natural and legitimate expressions of human nature and abstains from them as inherently evil: and when the assertion of other-worldliness takes the form of the condemnation as evil of certain orders of material things or of human interest and activity, it puts asunder what God has joined together. It makes unwarranted separations in human life, and it runs clean counter to the principle involved in the full doctrine of the Incarnation.

A popular modern cult, which carries to an extreme the denial of the material in nature and human life in the supposed interests of the spiritual, is found in Christian Science. In many respects indeed " our new religion "[11] is akin to Gnosticism. " Both draw a rigid line of distinction between matter and spirit, and set them in mutual conflict. Both are alike in seeing in matter no intellectual or spiritual value. Both ultimately stand, by virtue of their ultra-spiritual philosophy, in more or less patent antagonism to the principle of the Incarnation, which was the Divine proof of the high place of things material in the purpose of God."[12] Christian Science derived its strength and appeal, in the person of its leading figure and founder, by the contrast which it presented to the gloomy Calvinism which characterised the religion of the household and surroundings in which Mrs. Baker Eddy was brought up; proclaiming as it did the essential goodness and godlikeness of humanity in contrast with the doctrine of the total depravity of human nature and of arbitrary predestination characteristic of Calvinistic tradition. It may well too have been a natural reaction against

[11] *Our New Religion:* Herbert Fisher.
[12] *Ancient heresies in modern dress:* Radford, p. 199.

the prevailing philosophy of the period of its origin, which, in the light of the rapid advances of scientific knowledge and discovery characterising that period, tended to interpret the universe in terms of deterministic mechanism entirely ruling out the need and presence of the spiritual.

By an extreme reaction then against the religious and scientific outlook of the time and surroundings of its origin, Christian Science proclaimed not merely the predominance of the spiritual but the unreality of the material : and in its endeavour both in theory and practice to assert the primacy of spirit, it relegated the material world, including the human body and its experiences of sickness and death, to the realm of error and illusion. Its conception of God " the Father Mind," was such as to exclude any sort of creative relation between God and the external world : and in keeping with this conception, it could inevitably find no room for a real Incarnation. The Birth of Jesus was a " purely mental process," and the Christ is "the Divine principle of the Man Jesus" entering and possessing Him as the " Idea of God." It denies, therefore, the death of Jesus and regards the Resurrection not as a victory over actual death but as a proof that Jesus had not died. Similarly it proclaims that the worship which is in spirit and truth demands the entire exclusion of outward and material aids : and in its treatment of human ills, particularly sickness, suffering and death, it professes to surmount them by denying their reality and declaring them an illusion of mortal mind. Thus claiming the high title of Science it not only rules out the ministrations of the qualified physician but banishes the whole domain of phenomena, which form the data of scientific enquiry and discovery, to the limbo of unreality.   Claiming, too, the august name of Christian, it is a direct denial of the Christ of the Incarnation, with its implication of the creative relationship of God to the material world and of the redemption and consecration of the human body by the presence and power of the Divine : and in so far as it is consistent with its proclaimed beliefs, its ethical standard is one of aloofness from the claims and needs of average humanity entirely alien to the ethical spirit and teaching of the religion of the Incarnation.

It remains in the concluding part of this lecture to consider the Church's task in relation to the Incarnation, not merely in rejection of error but in exemplifying and applying the truth.   We have reviewed in turn some at least of those recurrent forms of thought and practice, non-sacramental and dualistic in tendency, which have appeared in Christian history and which involve in greater or less degree a denial of the Incarnation : and we have seen how the Church rejected them in turn, by methods effective if not always commendable. But the Church did more than refuse and repudiate error, whether of belief or practice, in relation to the Incarnation. It gave itself to the task of safeguarding, unfolding and applying in its fullest range the truth of the Incarnation.   This, indeed, and nothing else, has always been and is the primary office of the Church. It is the guardian of the full truth of the Incarnation, a trusteeship which from the apostolic age onwards it has watchfully discharged, on the ground, as we have seen, that with its maintenance and application ultimate values of human life and salvation are bound up. But the Church is far more than the chosen and authoritative guardian of the truth. It is itself its expression and living embodiment. In itself it carries on and extends the truth of the Incarnation. It, too, is sacramental in its being and nature. It, too, as the Christ, has two natures united in itself, it, too, is compounded of heaven and earth, of God and of humanity. It is indeed the visible expression of the divine-human Christ, His Body and the organ which represents Him and is identified with Him, and through which He carries on and completes His task and mission. The Church therefore belongs to the same order of being, and represents the same order of relationship between God and the material world, as the Christ Himself. It is itself a sacrament in the union which it embodies of divine and human values, and both within its own corporate life and in relation to the world of humanity it sets itself to apply the truth of the Incarnation and to give expression in every field of human life to the sacramental principle for which it stands.

For indeed it is not only the Church itself but its characteristic ordinances which partake of the sacramental character of the Incarnation as the ultimate reconciliation of that dualism, which recurs in thought and practice at widely separated epochs of

history, and the characteristic of which is to cut off
from each other God and the spiritual order on the
one hand and the world of nature and humanity on
the other.   Among these ordinances are the priesthood and the sacraments, each of which contains and
embodies the principle that the divine gifts to
humanity are mediated through human and
material channels.   Supreme among them stands the
Holy Eucharist, the perpetual visible pledge that in
Christ " heaven and earth have kissed each other,"
and that the divine is revealed in and mediated
through the natural and the material.   The Holy
Eucharist is the symbolic and perpetual vindication
of the claim and capacity of Christ to subdue, penetrate and transform the whole realm of human life
and of the natural order with the presence and
potency of the Divine : and in the light of the truth
of the Incarnation and pledged thereto by the
challenge of its central ordinance the Church has set
itself to the task of bringing under law to Christ and
of penetrating with, and subduing to, the spirit of
Christ not only all mankind but all realms of human
life and activity.

It has been, then, and is the main task of the
Church to embody and apply the truth of the Incarnation in its full range and implications.   For
this purpose it must not cramp or crush or supersede
human life and the natural expressions of the human
spirit.   It must attribute to them their full and rightful scope and value.   Yet equally must it bring them
under law to Christ.   It must declare, what indeed is
testified to by experience, that in and by themselves

they " fall short of the glory of God." In themselves they are stamped with the mark of non-attainment. So long as they remain on the natural level, and seek to attain their destiny without reference to any regulative order other than that of humanity, they fail of their destined perfection.   Governed by a law of their own, without regard to the wisdom which is from above, sooner or later they " perish in the using."   The lesson writ in large letters across the whole field of the world, of society as organised apart from God, is that of failure.   If the divine and specifically religious must not crush or obliterate the distinctive and legitimate values of human life and endeavour, no more are these complete or attain their goal except as redeemed and sanctified by the " bringing in of a better law," by the application to them of laws and principles derived from another and higher sphere.   The Kingdom of God is nothing else but the whole realm of human life as brought under the sovereignty of God, and, through this subjection, attaining its full glory and perfection. And it is for the Church Catholic, intensively within its own sphere, diffusively in the world without, to embody and express in this way the values of the Incarnation.

It is precisely to this function and task that the conception of the Church as a body is peculiarly applicable.   For the body is an organic unity characterised by a rich diversity : and the life and efficacy of the body is impaired just in so far as, on the one hand, any organ escapes from or repudiates control, and lives its life apart from and without reference to the whole, or, on the other hand, in so far as the head or centralised authority of the body crushes or supersedes the rightful scope and activity of its members : and the Church, like a body, is then most rich and living, when the unity of the whole is ministered to and supplied by the greatest possible variety of " gifts, ministrations, workings " offered in its service by its various members, corporate or individual. So historically the Church has stood out as then most truly an extension of the Incarnation and as most fully embodying the Spirit of Christ when it has subdued without suppressing, conquered without enslaving, indeed emancipated and perfected by its conquest, the whole realm of varied human life and activity.

It was this task which the Church set itself to and so largely accomplished in its earliest centuries. Witnessing for the faith for which it stood in the face of a pagan and largely hostile world, refusing to use any weapons but those of persuasion and spiritual power, itself often crushed by superior force, it yet acted as leaven, subduing to itself the lump of human society, as represented by the Roman civilisation of the period. " In the course of this brief space " (the second and third centuries of our era) " the Gospel penetrated successively the regions of domestic life, of speculation, of government, and at last was openly revealed as a power claiming complete sovereignty over the whole sum of human interests." [13] A change indeed came with the official recognition of Christianity by the Emperor and the

[13] *The two Empires:* Westcott, p. 1.

empire : and the Edict of Milan (A.D. 313) marked the beginning of a period in which the Church increasingly adopted the weapons and methods of the world for the extension of religion. The State and Empire used the Church as a main instrument of its unity and strength : and the Church resorted to the State, and to the force exercised by the State, to extend its influence and persecute its foes. Orthodoxy became the mark of subservience to the Emperor, heresy of the spirit and assertion of national independence. The increasing spirit of worldliness in the Church had its own inevitable recoil and protest, and drove those for whom the values of religion were primary into the desert and the wilderness, there to live the ascetic life alone or in community : while the loss so incurred of the finer spiritual element tended still further to the forfeiture by the Church of its distinctive character and its increasing subservience to political control.

In the West a different problem presented itself, viz. that of subduing to the yoke of Christ the barbarian invaders of the empire. The task was achieved, though here again at the cost, whether necessary or otherwise, of adopting force and wholesale methods of conversion as the weapons of the Church's victories. The overwhelming peril, as also the greatness of the task, demanded highly centralised authority, such as was found in the mediæval papacy. Much of the glamour and prestige of ancient Rome gathered round this august institution, which cemented as nothing else could the unity of the Church in the face of the disruptive forces, racial, national, religious, which threatened the break up of human society. Thus was fought the mediæval battle between the Church and the world out of which grew the conception of the Holy Roman Empire, the Emperor wielding the secular, and the Pope the spiritual weapon for the common end of establishing a uniformly Christian order of society throughout the civilised world. Here, again, and inevitably, much of the world invaded the Church, and the Papacy became increasingly a state among states, resorting to the weapons of the world, force and fraud, to secure its own aggrandisement. Here, too, the intenser light and life of religion was preserved in the monasteries, established remote from the world and on highly organised lines derived from the genius of S. Benedict. Throughout, then, this long period of a thousand years and more, the centuries in which the stamp of Christ was set on Western civilisation, the methods adopted of further-ing the cause of religion and securing its predomin-ance as the governing force of human life and society were often far removed from the spirit and teaching of Christ. Yet while the methods altered, the goal remained the same, that goal which, as we have seen, the Church as embodying and extending the principle involved in the Incarnation must consistently set itself to pursue, of subduing all men and all human life to the obedience of Christ. With all its failures, in this respect the mediæval Church did not fail. It " never failed to present the Kingdom of God as a visible society on earth in which every activity of man, every aspect of his individual and corporate life, was to be brought under the obedience of Christ. It never, in idea at least, suffered any district of life to fall outside its control, as if it could be carried on without reference to religion." [14]

Not only did it not fail: it succeeded. " In the Middle Ages the idea of the Kingdom of God, the idea of a united Christendom in which the whole life of mankind is under the sovereignty of the Lord Christ, not only becomes dominant as an idea, but also is realised, with whatever glaring imperfections, under our eyes." [15] It succeeded: indeed it succeeded too well. And the Renaissance and Reformation, indeed the whole modern era, represent in large measure a recoil from that excessive dominance of purely religious interests over the whole realm of human activity and the claims of the individual which characterised the Middle Ages. The typical doctrine of that epoch, that of Transubstantiation, with its denial of the substance of bread and wine in the Holy Sacrament and its attribution of sole reality to the Body and Blood of Christ, is representative of the tendency, in the interests of religion, to supersede and suppress the human and the natural, in every realm of life, which characterised that period. Speculation and scientific enquiry, art and literature, commerce and industry, all these and other realms of human activity craving the right and liberty of unhampered self-expression found themselves unduly cramped and confined by an all-dominant and controlling Church. The supposed interests of

[14] *Christ and Society*, Gore, p. 110.
[15] *op. cit.*, p. 118.

religion, and measures, particularly in the economic sphere, adopted to meet other times and circumstances were pressed unduly in their application to the surging forces of a new world. The result was a violent recoil from the dominance of an all-pervading religion : and " the Renaissance inaugurated a new movement for the assertion of legitimate human interests : and at one point after another the result has appeared in a demarcation of autonomous human spheres." [16] The process of emancipation of domains of human interest and activity set on foot with the Renaissance of the fifteenth and sixteenth centuries has gone forward since with increasing momentum : and the characteristic of the modern world is the secularisation of all such spheres, and their assertion of the claim to complete autonomy. The rise of nationalism in an ever acuter form reduced to an outworn anachronism the ideal of the Holy Roman Empire, and the secular State took and takes the place of the Church as the all-embracing, all-controlling factor in human life. Interests of State tended to become the all-regulative factor in policy. Religion was itself subordinated to ends of State, and the canon of justification in political action ceased to be determined by Christian principle and came to be fixed by reasons of State advantage only, as adjudged by those in power from time to time.

Moreover, over a large area, the Church acquiesced in the dominance of State interests, uncontrolled by ultimate religious sanction, and retired into its own specialised field. So again with business and

[16] *The Incarnate Lord:* Thornton, p. 265.

industry. " In the last six hundred years," says Lippmann, " the Churches have fought a losing battle against the emancipation of business from religious control." [17] The rise of modern large-scale industry and business took place at a period when the principle of *laissez faire* was accepted as governing political action with respect to this field, and the non-moral, non-Christian theory of enlightened self-interest and of unlimited competition had won general acceptance. The Church had made ineffectual efforts from time to time to apply principles applicable to a wholly different order of industry to business as it emerged in the modern era, but had neither the energy nor the inclination to think out and apply a new social and industrial Christian ethic applicable to the new conditions. The secularising process has invaded the private as well as the public life of society. Here, too, the religious bodies have fought a losing battle. " Here, too," adds Lippmann, " the dissolution of their authority has proceeded inexorably. They have lost their exclusive right to preside over marriage. They have not been able to maintain the dogma that marriage is indissoluble " [18] : and a concerted and well-thought-out effort is, as we shall see in more detail later, in process of being made to place the whole sphere of sexual relationship outside the area of religious sanction and control and to govern it by principles derived from other sources.

It is unnecessary to illustrate further the extent, in the great representative domains of human interest

---

[17] *A Preface to Morals,* p. 84.
[18] *op. cit.,* p. 88.

and activity, to which the process of emancipation from regard for religious sanction has gone, and an avowedly non-religious secular order of life has superseded it. The process has been carried out with most consistent thoroughness and on the widest scale in modern Soviet Russia, in which the Marxian conception of the sole dominance of economic considerations has been applied with relentless logical completeness, and the attempt is being made to regulate and govern the whole life of a vast and populous area of the globe on a basis which deliberately excludes regard for the spiritual from any place in governing human conduct and human affairs. But the same secularist spirit, as was emphasised from many quarters of the globe at the Jerusalem Missionary Conference of 1928, is characteristic of the whole of modern civilisation, which represents the endeavour of modern humanity to regulate its life by exclusively this-worldly considerations. Meanwhile, religion has been driven ever further from the wider fields of human affairs into an increasingly confined department of its own. It is " tempted to be content if it can express itself in a piety which is divorced from secular interests." [19] The time has come if ever to redress the balance, and while legitimate scope is given for rightful self-expression, in accordance with principles derived from their own domain, to all fields of human energy, yet to assert that those several domains only then can be unified and carried to completion if they are duly correlated with the eternal order and with principles derived

[19] Thornton, *op. cit.,* p. 265.

H

from a superhuman super-earthly sphere.   For "neither the supersession of human interests by religion, nor the emancipation of religion and human interests from one another can be adequate to the facts.   The true end of creation is represented adequately by neither movement.   Human life is neither simply autonomous and self-completing, nor is it doomed to be frustrated by some higher order of existence.   Its destiny is that it could be completed in God." [20]   Whether or how the balance can be redressed, and principles derived from the Incarnation be asserted throughout the whole order of modern civilisation, must be reserved for consideration till a later lecture.

[20] *Ib.,* p. 265.

SYNOPSIS.

THE Incarnation provides that transcendent principle of unity, through conformity with which can harmony alone be attained in the ethical sphere, individual and social. Our Lord set men free from the restrictive legalistic standard of morality prevalent in His day; and S. Paul carried the battle for moral liberty into the Gentile world. Here, however, the main issue was against an immorality of unrestraint and the substitution of licence for liberty. A similar protest is demanded to-day both against a Judaistic standard of external regulation and a Pagan standard of unrestrained licentiousness. More formidable than either to the Christian ethical standpoint is the attempt which is to-day being made, in responsible quarters, to find in human reflection and knowledge the sole basis of morality, and to exclude any form of supernatural sanction. Such an attempt is doomed to failure : for it is only by his entry into a higher moral order than the natural that man can attain to inner harmony and resolve the tension between himself and his neighbour. Such an entry is represented by baptism, which symbolises the two sides, negative and positive, of man's ethical transformation by incorporation into Christ, dead and risen again. The moral standard of the Incarnation can best be illustrated in the sphere of sex, which on the one hand has its own inherent worth, yet can run riot with human life and character, unless brought into obedience to Christ.

V. THE INCARNATION AND THE MORAL ORDER.

THE province of Ethics, considered from their practical aspect, is that of securing the harmonious adjustment of the inner life of man, and correspondingly of that life considered socially and in relation to his fellows. A development of individual character, which is yet subordinate and contributory to the welfare of the community, a closely-knit and compacted social order, which yet does not override the inalienable claims of individual self-expression, these are the twin excellencies which, mutually reconciled and mutually conditioned, a moral order adequate to the needs of humanity must show. It is our contention that neither result in the moral sphere can be realised on the natural level, and apart from reference to a supernatural order transcending and correlating the two spheres, individual and social, of the ethical life of man. On the natural level, as the broad face of modern civilisation reveals, there is a constant tension between the two. Individual attainment, as attainment is estimated, is too often purchased at the cost of the rights and interests of others, and without reference to the needs of the community as a whole: and conversely a highly organised social and industrial order is too often found only practicable at the cost of sacrificing the liberty and right of self-expression of the individual. It is only as both the individual and society are re-

born on a higher level, and re-fashioned by a " transcending principle of unity " other than and beyond
either, that the tension can be resolved and harmony
secured.   Such a principle is found and can only be
found in the Incarnation.   It provides the one
adequate basis of a moral order in which the highest
fruits of individual perfection are revealed alongside
a closely knit social order which neither overrides
nor is overridden by the moral claims of the individual.   " The two principles, whose mutual tension
cannot be resolved on their own level in the organic
series, are correlated in a new synthesis by transformation to the level of the new creation.   They
meet in the new humanity of Christ." [1]   It is the
task of this lecture to provide in some measure the
background, particularly in the New Testament on
the one hand and in modern life on the other, against
which this moral outcome of the Incarnation can
best be viewed.

It is then maintained that the Incarnation is the
ground and basis of a new order of life, both individual and social, and one higher than that which is
possible to unaided nature.   In itself it is a revelation
of the perfection of manhood, sinless and complete.
It belongs to the very nature of the Incarnation that
in it manhood is not superseded or overridden but
revealed in its fulness and maturity.   Nor is it in a
new code of ordinances superseding the Mosaic, or
again even in the teaching and example of Christ,
that the new order of human life is constituted, but
in His Person.   His message of the Kingdom illus-

[1] *The Incarnate Lord:*   Thornton, p. 277.

trates indeed, from the standpoint both of individual character and of social life, what form under historic circumstances that new order of life is to take. But it is in Him that the new level of manhood and of human life is constituted, and from Him that it derives its origin. His teaching supplies a " pattern of sound words " according to which human character and life is to be re-built. But the spring and secret and source of that new potentiality of human character and life is Himself, and His indwelling Spirit. That Spirit or mind of Christ operates upon and moulds and transforms the individual and his character, as he is taken up into the new order of redeemed humanity. On this level the conflict between flesh and spirit is resolved, the lower nature being subdued and brought into obedience by the presence of a power which, while entering from above and beyond, yet operates within man by identification with his spiritual nature. " The problem of self-harmonisation was in principle solved by the indwelling of the Holy Spirit, which ensured the ultimate triumph of the principle of spirit over all lower tendencies and routines of habit in the spiritual organism of man." [2] But it is not merely in the negative deliverance of the spirit and the spiritual principle in man from the enthralment of the flesh that the new level and order of life in Christ is manifested. " It is a positive re-building of character on larger and more generous lines than any attainment of character which could be possible outside of the Spirit's action in the new order." [3]

[2] Thornton, *op. cit.*, p. 275.   [3] *Ib.*, p. 275.

Natural endowments and capacities, the pagan virtues, are not destroyed or superseded, but carried up to and transformed on the new level. At the same time new virtues and excellencies of character appear which are the distinctive fruits of the Spirit : and the true type and order of spiritual manhood is revealed, in which " the principle of individuality is recognised, treasured, and brought into conformity with a new rhythm of development." [4]

But the moral emancipation and achievement so effected on the level of the Incarnation is not in the individual only. The transformation of individual character and life is not wrought apart from the brotherhood. " The Apostolic writings know nothing of an individual development which is apart from or outside the new social fellowship, the new community of which Christ is the Head." [5] In the Christ and by the indwelling Spirit of Christ there is found not only the spring and source of individual growth and attainment, but " a new sociological principle," by conforming with which individual character comes to full expression and fruition through membership in a renewed social order. In the light of this principle graces and virtues are regarded not merely as individual endowments, but as gifts given " to profit withal " [6] and for the enrichment of the life of the body ; while sins are thought of less as breaches of external commandments than as anti-social acts, transgressions against the spirit of brotherhood. The whole background

[4] *op. cit.*, p. 274.
[5] *op. cit.*, p. 276.

[6] 1 Cor. xii. 7.

of S. Paul's ethical teaching, as indeed that of our Lord, is social. It is in reference to the brother and the brotherhood that the new ethical order in Christ finds expression and application. The conception of the Church as the Body of Christ, so suggestive in many directions, points to an ethical order in which individual excellencies are subordinate to, and find their fitting place and scope in, the new social order, apart from which they cannot attain to full fruition : and it is on this level, and this level alone, that of the Incarnation, that the mutual and often jarring claims of the individual and of society are met and satisfied in a higher synthesis. " The two principles, whose mutual tension cannot be resolved on their own level in the organic series, are correlated in a new synthesis by transformation to the level of the new creation. They meet in the new humanity of Christ." [7]

The supreme revelation of the Old Testament was, as we have already seen, that of the moral transcendence of the God of Israel. If God was One, yet more was He righteous and claimed righteousness of those who would approach Him. The constant protest of the prophets is against those non-moral conceptions of God, habitual in the surrounding peoples, which in Israel also found expression in ceremonial observances divorced from requirements of conduct and character. " To do justly, to love mercy, to walk humbly with God," such was the divine requirement answering to the divine self-revelation. Moreover, this ethical response to the

[7] Thornton, *op. cit.,* p. 277.

revelation of the Divine character, as voiced by the prophets, was couched almost wholly in social terms. The individual had not yet come into his own, as a unit of ultimate moral value. It was still Israel, as the people of God, on which the eyes of the prophets were set: and it was pre-eminently those virtues required in a right adjustment of social relationships on which the prophets laid stress. Yet however far short they fell of attributing to the individual his ultimate worth and capacity of attainment, it was their supreme achievement to have secured the final recognition of a moral and social order as the primary answer and return which was required by the whole course of divine self-revelation. "Be ye holy, for I am Holy," is the supreme command of the Old Covenant, and the ideal which throughout was held up to Israel as a whole by its highest and most spiritual minds. It was a high and difficult ideal; and it failed of attainment in the Israel of the Old Covenant. Indeed, the conditions of its attainment were wanting: for its attainment demanded a new "passing over" of the Hebrew people, and their acceptance of and reception into a new and better covenant than the Mosaic: and that final "passing over" as a people they refused. Instead they sought attainment of the ideal of a holy people within the domain of law. The post-exilic Judaic community was pre-eminently the people of the Torah. A standard of life, social and individual, wholly regulated by divine ordinance, was accepted: and the scribes of Israel sought to provide, through a multitude of minute regulations, a hedge about the law by which its transgressions could be avoided and every detail of life brought under obedience to God. It was a magnificent attempt at theocratic government : but it riveted on the people's necks a yoke of moral bondage, which cramped and circumscribed their character and conduct, and blinded them to the reality of moral distinctions. It created over against a "people accursed," because they knew not the law, a spiritual aristocracy which alone knew and could know and keep it. It set minor ceremonial regulations on a level with great moral precepts, and it issued in a restrictive standard of denial and prohibition utterly subversive of moral growth, individual or social.

It was from the bondage of this rigid legalistic standard of morality, the privilege of the few and the despair of the many, that our Lord set men free. His task and achievement as teacher was to lift from men's shoulders those "heavy burdens and grievous to be borne," [8] which the accepted religious authorities had laid upon them. He looked round on a social order, the cement of which was a legal code of fixed and minute regulations, and within which the righteous man was he who fulfilled most scrupulously the ordinances so prescribed, and with the assertion of a unique authority He broke through the cordon of rules and regulations circumscribing men's lives, and asserted the claims of humanity as overriding the letter of the law. He told His hearers that they could have no part or lot in the new order, unless their righteousness "exceeded the righteousness of

[8] Mth. xxiii. 4.

the Scribes and Pharisees."[9]   Their standard of
conduct was to overflow the canalised limits within
which the recognised moral standard moved.   They
were no longer to be content with a standard of
measured obligation, of limited moral liability.   Forgiveness, love, service, were to know no measure;
and as with the standard of social obligation, so with
that of individual character.   Righteousness in the
individual was no longer to be measured by a
standard of exact observance.   It was to be based
on nothing short of the perfection of God.   Rejection
of the old restrictive morality, with its false distinctions and judgments, is expressed in its most
emphatic form in the sustained prophetic denunciation of the Scribes and Pharisees which S. Matthew
puts in our Lord's mouth:[10]   while on the positive
side the Sermon on the Mount[11] represents those
sayings, gathered and arranged and leading up to
their   tremendous   climax,   which   embody   the
principles of the new morality, principles based on
a new relationship of man to God, and of man to his
neighbour.

Our Lord's prophetic task, then, was one of moral
emancipation.   Yet it was a higher and harder and
not a lower standard of character and conduct to
which He summoned.   For a law which fettered and
bound He gave a sovereign " law of liberty " [12] in
the understanding and obedience of which was
blessedness to be found.   The sources and sanctions
of obedience to that new moral order we shall con-

---

[9] Mth. v. 20.

[10] Mth. xxiii.

[11] Mth. v.—vii.

[12] James i. 25, ii. 12.

sider shortly. So much at least is clear, that the moral standard proclaimed by Jesus, whether in reference to the individual or to the social order, is wholly removed from those later developments of legalism within which the great ethical appeals of Old Testament prophecy had become bound and circumscribed. The tendency towards a legalistic standard of morality is strongly rooted in human nature. It is easier, makes less claim on thought, judgment and effort, than a morality of freedom. The standard survived in the Judaistic school of the Christian Church. Attempts were made to rivet it on Gentile believers, and so to secure a triumph for Jewish propagandism: and much of S. Paul's polemic, particularly in the earlier period of his missionary enterprise, was directed against those zealous apostles of the Judaising school, which sought to " entangle again in a yoke of bondage " [13] those pagan believers who had been brought into the school of Christ.

But the battle for moral liberty was fought and won. On the Gentile field it was not for liberty, but against its abuse that S. Paul was compelled to direct his chief efforts. Here the peril was not a morality of restrictive legalism, but an immorality of licentiousness and unrestraint. On this field liberty might all too easily be used as a " cloak of maliciousness." [14] Again and again the Apostle draws a vivid picture of the moral degradation characteristic of the Græco-Roman seaboard cities in which he had planted churches. His Christian converts were

[13] Gal. v. 1.   [14] 1 Pet. ii. 16.

largely drawn from a society which had thrown over all moral inhibitions, and had run riot in obedience to the passions and lusts of the natural man. " Fornication, and all uncleanness "[15] were habitual; and sexual licence was not only rampant, but was practised under the sanction of religion. There was thus the constant peril, as is abundantly evidenced by the mission field to-day also, of Christian converts slipping back, under pressure of popular opinion and practice, into the wild extravagance of moral unrestraint which they had repudiated in their baptism : and S. Paul had constantly to impress upon them that Christian liberty was not licence, and that it involved for them a definite severance from their former manner of life and a new standard of moral obligation conformable with the fact that they had " put on Christ."

There are two standards of conduct then, as evidenced by the New Testament, against both of which the religion of the Incarnation is a protest. The one is the standard of impersonal law, the rigid static standard of compliance with external rule and regulation. The other is the standard of unrestraint, of yielding to the passions and impulses of the natural man. The protest on either side is as necessary to-day as in the first century of our era. The Judaistic standard of external restraint and prohibition is still inculcated in circles which have inherited the Puritan tradition, a standard which, while borrowed from the law, is wrongly vested with the authority of the Gospel. Indeed, partly

[15] Eph. v. 3. Cp. iv. 19; Coloss. iii. 5.

perhaps through the prominent place which the
Decalogue occupies in Christian instruction and worship, it is with this standard that in the popular
mind Christian morality is largely identified. It is
thought of, as Walter Lippmann pictures it,[16] as a
morality based on a conception of the world and of
human life as under the ordering and governance of
a heavenly King who issues His commands, and
attaches rewards and punishments to the response,
of obedience or transgression, made to His commands. It is against this arbitrary and capricious
standard of morality, resting on a supposed supernatural sanction, that the modern world is in revolt :
and in recoil from a moral standard based on external authority it is only too apt to regard as the
only alternative a standard wholly unrestrained, of
non-repression and of following the dictates of
nature, the caprice or desire or passion which is
uppermost. From the Puritanic standard of con-
vention and custom prescribed by authority, human
or divine, there is a relapse to the antinomian
standard of modern paganism. The latter, however, brings its own sharp correction. For both for
the individual and in the social sphere, an emancipation which finds expression in unrestrained licence,
so far from achieving harmony and freedom, only
ends in establishing a far more galling bondage than
the external restraints repudiated.

This is readily recognised : nor is it with this form
of revolt from a morality based on religious sanction
that the religion of the Incarnation has mainly to

[16] *A Preface to Morals.*   See pp. 51ff.

contend. Its more formidable opponent is a clearly thought-out and expressed conception of human character and conduct, based on the deliberate principle of excluding any reference to a transcendent order outside the range of natural humanity. Recent years have witnessed a sustained attempt to abandon any sanction for morality higher than that of human reflection and reason, and to seek and to find a basis for it wholly within the natural order. Human conduct, so it is concluded, is to be based upon nature as interpreted by biology and psychology without reference to any higher principle. Lippmann's *Preface to Morals,* for example, is a sustained attempt " to formulate a mode of life by which ordinary men, thrown upon their own resources, can find their way without supernatural rules, commands, punishments and compensations." [17] This task, he maintains, is inevitable in view of the radical " irreligion of the modern world," and its complete repudiation of authority in the religious and moral spheres. A new foundation for morality must be found, in default of any recourse to supernatural sanction, within man himself. Within himself man must, if at all, find a means of co-ordinating and unifying his conflicting desires and impulses. Within himself and for himself he must develop to maturity. Here is the new religion, as " the art and the theory of the internal life of man, so far as it depends on the man himself, and on what is permanent in the nature of things." [18]

[17] *op. cit.,* p. 203.
[18] *op. cit.,* p. 195 (quoted from A. N. Whitehead).

Such must be the religion of those who are to " find the tests of righteousness wholly within human experience." [19]   It is the aim of " high religion," as so conceived, to carry into the region of morality and everyday conduct the spirit and methods of science, that spirit of impersonal disinterestedness which does not seek to mould the world to human desire, but to take it as it is, to understand it, and to adjust life to it.   Thus " pure science is high religion incarnate," [20] and he is the perfect man, practising the religion of the spirit, who " follows the long and difficult process of learning and training to adjust his wishes to the world.   If he succeeds he is mature.   If he is mature, he is once again harmonious with the nature of things.   He has virtue : and he is happy." [21] Here, then, is no mere morality of unrestraint, while yet there is an entire rejection of an external standard of authority, and indeed of any reference to a transcendent order.   Here is an attempt to build character and conduct on a basis of science, through the study and reduction to law of man's inner life, and the practice of those habits of discipline which psychology has revealed as effective for the purpose, whether for the individual or in the social sphere. Such is the scientific Pelagianism of to-day, the attempt to build up a moral order, a standard of conduct and character, on a basis of inductive knowledge and without reference to anything above and beyond it : and in its claim to the self-sufficiency of human nature, assisted by acquired knowledge, to

[19] *op. cit.*, p. 137.
[20] *op. cit.*, p. 239.
[21] *op. cit.*, p. 180.

I

achieve its own moral destiny, it is in line with those early formulations of Christological doctrine which pressed the humanity of Christ to the extent of dividing His Person. It was not for nothing that Pelagius was condemned along with Nestorius at the Council of Ephesus.

It is however with the modern attempt to " find the tests of righteousness wholly within human experience " and to build up a moral order on that basis alone that we are primarily concerned. The value of the exact and detailed study given, particularly in recent years, to the structure and working of the inner life of man, is beyond question. For the right ordering and conduct of life must at least in part depend on the knowledge of the facts of life, and of the elements of our complex nature which need to be unified and adjusted to their true ends. Yet that very study and its results, so far from providing a satisfying basis of conduct and character on the natural level, only serve to bring into clearer relief the need of reference to a transcendent moral order, in order to harmonise and resolve the tension which prevails between the elements of man's nature and between the individual and society. Within the natural order, and within man as a member of that order, no finality can be reached. Nor can such finality be attained, unless room is found for a " foundation of conduct outside and above the natural plane in the will of a transcendent God." [22] Moral effort must be thought of, as Professor Taylor has recently pointed out, as " a movement of

[22] *Conduct and the Supernatural:* Thornton, p. 268.

response, elicited and sustained throughout by an antecedent outgoing movement from the side of the Eternal." [23]   Thus morality " involves the supernatural . . . as its environment and daily nutriment " [24] : and the moral life is " a regeneration and remaking of the self in the likeness of a contemplated Eternal Good." [25]   Behind and within all moral striving and moral attainment there is an " initiative of the eternal," a movement of grace by response and conformity to which man can alone attain his supreme good, which is " something to be won and therefore something communicated and derivative." [26]

So long then as man seeks to achieve his moral destiny on his own level alone, however far aided by the fruit of scientific study, he fails to attain inner harmony or to resolve the tension between himself and his neighbour.   Non-attainment and frustration are the inevitable results of attempts to work out human salvation within the limits of human effort alone.   For on the one hand there is within man a disharmony and moral impotence of which he becomes only the more conscious as he strives in his own strength to overcome it : and on the other he is conscious of a transcendent order of goodness, ever beyond and above him, the attainment of which eludes his own best endeavours, yet in the attainment of which he can alone find ultimate satisfaction.   Hence the incompetence of man to save himself by the effort of his

---

[23] *Faith of a Moralist*, p. 14.   [25] *op. cit.*, p. 119.
[24] *op. cit.*, p. 230.   [26] *op. cit.*, p. 124.

own will or by knowledge alone, and the consequent need of a " passing over " into a new and higher order of existence in which man is taken out of himself and achieves individual and social harmony by an experience which transcends the limits of unaided nature. It is only as he is taken up into, and born anew in, a new and higher order, transcending the natural, and himself as a member of the natural order, that he can attain to inner harmony and maturity, and resolve the tension between himself and his neighbour.

It must, however, be remembered that that new and higher order through incorporation into which man can alone find his true level and achieve his destiny is wholly different from an external system of legal restraint. It is the supposed externalism and arbitrariness of the religious background to conduct against which the modern recoil is chiefly directed. The new and transcendent basis of conduct, however, on which alone moral and social harmony can be attained, though it is other than and from beyond the natural order, yet takes shape as an inner and first-hand experience, which does not cramp or destroy but redeems and transforms the natural. It is " the experience of Christ entering in and abiding in the soul." [27] It is that principle, that " law of the Spirit of life," [28] which, so far from being identical with the rigidity of legal restraint, emancipates man's soul from such bondage, as also from the corresponding bondage of his own unrestrained passions and lusts.

[27] *Conduct and the Supernatural:* Thornton, p. 171.
[28] Rom. viii. 2.

In this connection the symbolism and significance of baptism are of primary importance. In the teaching of S. Paul baptism is the moment, whether referred to directly or by implication, at which a decisive break is made with the old life, on the natural level, and entry is effected into a new and higher order. It is the sacrament of participation in the death and resurrection of Jesus; and it is by spiritual conformity to these historic events that the new order of life is constituted which is the ground of moral and social attainment. It is not primarily by the following of Jesus' example, or the practice of His teaching, as given in the Gospels, that life on the Christian level is constituted. These indeed constitute the classic and authoritative expression, under a certain set of historic circumstances, of the Christian order of life. Their significance and value, however, can only be apprehended by those who are already " in Christ." It is for the redeemed and regenerate community that the teaching of the Sermon on the Mount holds good and provides a normal type or standard of life. Indeed, the Incarnation itself and its moral values only spring to light and are apprehended in their full significance, as men are taken up into Christ and incorporated into a new and higher order of life than the natural. It is, then, from the standpoint of those who have been made like the Christ in His Death and Resurrection, that the Christian moral and social order is to be viewed. It is constituted in Him, and in particular by conformity to His Death and Resurrection. Thus it has a negative and a positive aspect. On the one hand its note is that of denial, renunciation, crucifixion. It is a dying daily to "the old man, which is corrupt according to the deceitful lusts." [29] Here, indeed, is the true asceticism. It is the practice of those habits of discipline and mortification, by which conformity to the death of Christ is increasingly attained, and "the flesh with the passions and the lusts thereof" [30] is increasingly "crucified" in the interest of the spirit and the spiritual order of life. Such asceticism is wholly removed from that Gnostic attitude towards created existence which condemns the body and nature as inherently evil. It is rather the practice of that detachment from and abnegation of the lower range of existence, including not only things sinful but things in themselves morally neutral, in order to give scope to the full assertion of the new and dominating principle of life.

For the negative aspect of the Christian moral order is not the whole. If that order is constituted by conformity to the death of Christ, so also is it by conformity to His resurrection. Indeed, the one is the ground and condition of the other. If Baptism embodies and symbolises on the one hand a death to sin, so also does it on the other a new birth to righteousness. And it is life lived in conformity with the risen life of Jesus that constitutes the essential factor of the Christian moral order. Here on the level of the risen life of Jesus man is a "new creature." On this level all values are transvaluated. Here old things are passed away, and are become

[29] Eph. iv. 22.   [30] Gal. v. 24.

new. On this level a new sacredness attaches to the whole created order, including the body and physical life of man. Here all things are his to enjoy, as seen and approached and possessed in Christ. For it is in this sacramental aspect, and as itself consecrated and taken up on to the level of spirit, that the order of nature can at last and only be rightly approached and rightly enjoyed. From the standpoint of conformity to the risen and ascended Lord, all nature is itself seen as born anew, is constituted on a new and higher level, and becomes the rightful environment and possession of regenerate humanity. So with character and moral attainment in the individual sphere. On this level a new order and possibility of moral capacity looms into view and is effectually constituted. It is on this level that the type of character adumbrated in the Beatitudes and acted out to the full by our Lord is seen as the natural and normal expression of the indwelling Spirit of Christ. Old virtues regarded as primary on the lower natural plane are transformed, or relegated to a lower level, as the skeleton framework within which the higher qualities can be cultivated and attained. Here, too, new excellencies of character are revealed, which, whether new names be coined for them, or old names used, are yet those peculiar graces which adorn and evidence the presence of renewed and regenerate humanity.

Finally, it is on this level that the old tension between the individual and the social order is resolved. From the standpoint of conformity to the Death and Resurrection of Jesus, the term brotherhood takes on a new and higher meaning. The sins and offences committed are seen not as breaches of a commandment given from without, but as anti-social offences, as breaches of the brotherhood, as acts of despite to the indwelling Spirit. Here, indeed, on this level, a new order of social life is constituted, and with it a new conception of neighbourly obligation. Here the term love comes into its own in its full length and breadth and height and depth. It is on this the regenerate level of redeemed humanity, reconstituted in Christ, that both in area and depth old standards of neighbourly obligation are obliterated, and a brotherhood is constituted which knows no boundary short of humanity, no limits of obligation short of the sacrifice of life for another. It is from this new and higher level, of conformity to the Death and Resurrection of Christ, and of the indwelling Spirit, that the old writing of frustration and non-attainment is obliterated. It is on this level that harmony is reached within each and within the social order. It is from this standpoint that the New Testament becomes an open book, and its teaching is apprehended in its true perspective. Here is that new life in Christ, constituted in Baptism and nourished in the Eucharist, which is the crown and sum of man's moral attainment, that new and higher order of life within which his moral cravings are satisfied, and his moral destiny is achieved.

It may be well in conclusion to illustrate what has been said on the moral standard which is based on the Incarnation, from the sphere of sex and of sex relationships. For here is not merely one sphere among many which could be chosen as the testing ground and touchstone of Christian morality. So pre-eminent among the spheres of human conduct is the sexual, that to it the terms moral and immoral have come to be applied in a specialised and not only in a general sense. Certainly it is by its success or failure in this sphere that the Christian, as any other ethical standard, must stand or fall. For with a right or wrong direction and control of sex goes very largely the determination of character. If this element is left unregulated or misdirected there is at once involved for the whole man moral peril and indeed the risk of moral disaster : while if sex is brought under the domain of the spirit, it is more than probable that the whole nature and character will be similarly ruled. S. James asserts that the tongue is the organ which governs the body, and that " if any stumbleth not in word, the same is a perfect man, able to bridle the whole body also." [31] If this be true of the tongue and of speech, it is yet more true of the sexual instinct and its expression that here lies the touchstone of moral mastery and of moral attainment.

For here pre-eminently are present those two factors which we have seen to be characteristic of human nature and of human life as a whole. For here on the one hand is an element of human nature which claims recognition, which has its own inde-feasible worth, and which is only denied or ignored

[31] James iii. 2.

at the cost of moral shipwreck. Sex has its essential place in the economy of human life, as a factor which insistently demands rightful scope and expression. Yet on the other hand there is no element of human nature which stands in greater need of being brought under the domain of a higher law, of being lifted from the natural to the supernatural level. For there is no element, which, exercised within its own natural limits and indulged on its own natural level, is more calculated to run riot with the whole man, indeed with whole races of men. For it is in the sexual sphere, so it would appear, that is largely to be found the source of that moral degradation and degeneracy which is characteristic of primitive peoples.[32] Certainly regarded in this light the words used by S. James of the tongue are equally true of sex, that it " is a fire : the world of iniquity among our members, which defileth the whole body, and setteth on fire the wheel of nature, and is set on fire by hell." [33] Hence essential as sex is as an element in human nature, claiming recognition and possessing its own high value, it needs as much as or more than any other factor to be brought under law to God, to be " not merely viewed from the animal standpoint," but " lifted to the level of the high spiritual interests of life." [34]

Yet such control does not mean suppression or extinction, still less the condemnation of the sex instinct as in itself inherently evil. It is " a God-

[32] Cp. *Le Non-Civilisé et Nous:* Raoul Allier, pp. 262—267.
[33] James iii. 6.
[34] Lambeth Conference, 1930 (Report, p. 85).

given factor in the life of mankind, and its functions are therefore essentially noble and creative." [35]   To condemn it or suppress it as sinful is only to pervert it from those proper functions and to ensure a perilous moral recoil.   In line with Gnostic dualism and the view that the body and its organs and functions are evil, schools of thought and practice within and without the Church have risen, which have sought an eradication of the sex instinct and desire by a rigorous and merciless system of ascetic discipline. In concupiscence, considered not as sexual licence but as the sex instinct itself, they have seen the root of all evil.   It is not, however, by its suppression or condemnation that a right control is to be exercised over and a right direction given to the sex instinct.   Nor, on the other hand, is the instinct to be left to the governance of unbridled desire.   It was this attitude to sex, that of licentious indulgence and unrestraint, which, as we have seen, was characteristic of pagan life in the great cities of the Græco-Roman Empire of the first century and against which S. Paul so earnestly warns his converts :   and it is this attitude of ungoverned indulgence, of regarding and treating sex as within the scope of individual caprice and passion that is equally prevalent to-day and is a main example of that individualistic recoil from all forms of objective authority which is characteristic of our age.   It is not in its undue suppression, nor yet in its ungoverned indulgence that that approach to sex and sex relationship is to be found which is characteristic of the religion of the Incarnation.

[35] *op. cit.*

Different from either of these solutions of the problem, yet equally remote from the Christian, is that to which we have already alluded in connection with the modern attitude to matters of moral concern generally. It is that the sex question is to be solved in the light of modern knowledge and experience, and in entire disregard of spiritual or supernatural sanction. Such is the attitude adopted by Mr. Bertrand Russell in his *Marriage and Morals,* and by Mr. Walter Lippmann in his *Preface to Morals.* These and other writers bring to bear upon the question the knowledge which psychology and allied sciences has made possible in this sphere, and claim that by such knowledge aided by common sense and experience the best way out can be found from the tangled problem which sex presents. It is not to be denied that the knowledge thus gained has proved of immense worth, and that sex education of the right kind in the light of such knowledge is an essential factor in the solution of the problem. Yet " the intellect moves nothing," and knowledge of the facts and functions of sex in itself is of no avail against the disruptive and volcanic forces which it contains within it, unless, coupled with the knowledge, there is given also a power of control and co-ordination, a power which is only to be found by subservience to the law of the Spirit, and by raising the whole nature to a higher than the natural level.

Hence, not least, but above all in matters of sex and sexual relationship, and particularly as the latter finds expression in marriage, the imperative need of bringing in that something more, that higher law,

that " other worldly love," which without suppressing or denying the natural instinct, yet transforms
it and lifts it into conformity with higher claims
and demands than those which belong to the level of
nature.   Here, as in other spheres, it is the part of
the Holy Spirit to take of the things of man and
make them Christ's.   Here, as elsewhere, it is in the
sacramental principle, which finds its supreme
sanction and example in the Incarnation, and by
which the natural is transformed by union with the
divine, that is to be found that approach to the fact
and problem of sex that can alone meet the need.
Herein not least the religion of the Incarnation has
proved its finality, and stands unique among the
religions of history, that accepting the fact of sex
and recognising its place and worth in the life of
man, it has redeemed it from animality and made it
the channel and vehicle of the highest spiritual value.
Capable if misused at the personal caprice of the
individual of making utter havoc of his moral
capacities, and indeed of the social order, it may also
if brought under the domain of the Spirit of Christ
prove a main factor in raising the whole character
to the spiritual level.   For sex and sexual relationship are not there to be denied or impoverished but
to be brought into conformity with the will and
purpose of God : and it is as they are viewed in
relation to the kingdom of eternal values and made
subject to higher ends than that of their own
satisfaction on the physical level that harmonious
adjustment of the inner nature is won and moral
mastery and maturity secured.

SYNOPSIS.

THE truth of the Incarnation once acknowledged becomes finally regulative in the spheres both of thought and of character and conduct: and the supreme task of the Church is to apply the truth over the whole area of human life. To-day on the widest scale the spheres of the secular and the sacred confront each other as separate interests. Yet each suffers from isolation, and each needs to be supplemented by the other. Such a synthesis can alone be effected in the light of the Incarnation and the sacramental order based upon it. In this task the Anglican Church through her characteristic tradition and outlook, has a special responsibility and opportunity. During the epoch of the Reformation the Church of England asserted its position against post-Tridentine Rome on the one hand, and Calvinistic Puritanism on the other, and through the work of Hooker and others stood out as the champion of spiritual liberty and of the rights of humanity as against the eternal decrees. In contrast with the evangelical revival, with its main emphasis on individual conversion, the Oxford Movement laid primary stress on the Incarnation, with its implications of the corporate life and sacramental order of the Church. It restored to the Church a sense of its place and mission in Christendom. Its missionary enterprise on the one hand, and its attitude to reunion on the other are leading illustrations of the loyalty of the Anglican Church to the principles of the Incarnation. The Eucharist is a perpetual renewal of the Incarnation.

VI. THE INCARNATION AND THE ANGLICAN TRADITION.

THE Incarnation is the union of Godhead and manhood in the Person of Christ. It affirms in the form of concrete fact a unity where human thought has for the most part seen only a sharp antithesis. For human thought there has in the main been an unresolved dualism between God and the created order, the spiritual and the material, eternity and the time series. In the Incarnation that dualism stands resolved, and factors seemingly irreconcilable are seen embraced in a sacramental union. Moreover, that synthesis once recognised and accepted becomes a new starting point for human thought on the nature and destiny of the world. The truth of the Incarnation is determinant and regulative for all enquiry into the ultimate constitution of things. It becomes the test and standard of truth. In the light of the Word made Flesh all earlier or later thinking about God and the world, and the relation between the two, receives its correction or refutation, its fulfilment or corroboration. Above all, it is the corroboration and fulfilment of that presentation of the problem, which, not in the form of abstract speculation, but in that of a concrete historical record, the Old Testament contains. Similarly the Incarnation throws its light forward. In the sphere of thought and enquiry it is the final touchstone of the truth of any theory of the world offered by science and philosophy : and it is just because as we have seen, the organic theory or modern philosophy in a high degree both illuminates and is illuminated by the fact of the Incarnation, indeed involves in itself that very synthesis that receives its supreme exemplification in the Incarnation, that it may be taken to represent a marked advance in the quest of ultimate truth.

But the Incarnation is equally determinant in the sphere of conduct and character. It includes, sanctions and gives scope to those values for which room must be found in human life at its highest and therefore at its truest. Indeed the Church was largely guided, as we have seen, in its formulation of the doctrine of Christ, not so much by considerations of logical exactitude as by those ultimate factors of life and experience which in practice had been found to be mediated by Christ. No such formulation could gain ultimate acceptance by the Church unless, at whatever cost to the demands of the axioms of current thought, it included and provided for those elements which were the ground and basis of Christian experience : and just as that experience was a determinant factor in the development of the doctrine of Christ, so the truth of the Incarnation, of the union of Godhead and Manhood in the Person of Christ, once revealed and accepted in its fulness, is finally regulative for human conduct and character, the standard and possibility of life at its best. In affirming the perfect and complete humanity of Christ, the Incarnation is the ultimate recognition of the worth of human nature, and sanctions and embraces all those values of life, character and expression which are proper to humanity on the natural level. It is the standing condemnation of any attitude of religious thought and practice, which involves the supersession or frustration of such values. But equally does it condemn any attitude which asserts the self-sufficiency of human nature within its own limits. For the Incarnation affirms also the perfect Godhead of Christ, and in doing so reveals that the goal, destiny and perfection of human life cannot be attained within its own limits and on its own level, but only by union with the divine. For man belongs to the organic series, and though he is its sum and crowning point, he is marked by that imperfection and non-attainment, that need of being re-fashioned by a higher transcending principle of unity, which belongs to every stage of the series : and it is only as manhood is taken into God, that the goal is reached and not mankind only but the whole organic order is revealed in its full significance.

Thus, in Christ, humanity and the whole natural order is not superseded, is indeed preserved, yet is also transformed and recreated on the higher supernatural level. It is as he is re-born in Christ, taken up in Him on to that higher supernatural level, that man at last and alone comes into his own. On that level he is a new creation, and all things for him are made new. New ranges and possibilities of character and conduct come into view, and while his life on the one hand is a daily dying to sin, of sternest ascetic discipline in the task of subduing his lower nature, it is also a daily new birth to righteousness,

K

a going forward to those heights of moral attainment, of joy, of love, of holiness, which are the goal of his striving and the fruits of the Spirit. Similarly in the light of the Incarnation, and for those taken up into union with Christ, all things are theirs to enjoy by a new title of possession. They know how to use without abusing the world of natural things around them, which indeed is itself seen in Christ as sharing in man's redemption. For the Incarnation represents the hallowing of the persons and things of everyday life, the transformation of the commonplace by contact with the Divine : and though " we see not yet all things subjected to Him,"[1] yet in promise and potentiality there is contained within the historic fact of the Word made Flesh the subduing to Christ of all mankind and the totality of human life. Here is the supreme task of the Catholic Church, in guarding and applying in its full range and significance the truth of the Incarnation; a task which is not complete until the whole order of human society, and all departments of human life, interest and activity are brought into obedience to Christ and transformed by His Spirit.

Here is the supreme task of to-day : for to-day, on the broad field of human society, as perhaps never before, religion and everyday life, the sacred and the secular, are held apart in rigid distinction from each other : and as such the civilisation of to-day represents a defiance and denial of the truth and implications of the Incarnation. Two spheres of interest and activity confront us, each with its own

[1] Heb. ii. 8.

rights and claims, yet standing over against each other, often antagonistic to and exclusive of each other, the world of nature and external interests on the one hand, and the world of things unseen, of spiritual values and reality on the other. The representatives of the one sphere are apt to go their way without regard to those of the other, content to consider their world in each case as complete and self-contained, and in no need of supplementing from the other side. Indeed, even within the limits of the individual life, it is not uncommon that the natural or secular interests on the one hand, and the spiritual or religious on the other, should be kept in separate compartments, without any consciousness of the dualism thus created, and without any attempt at bringing the one to terms with the other. Yet neither for thought nor for life is it tolerable that the two domains should be kept for ever apart. If human life, whether that of the individual or of society, is to be rounded and complete, the two independent spheres of the sacred and the secular must be reconciled, and a synthesis found within which the one will supplement and complete the other.

It may be well to set in clearer relief the contrast between the two spheres of the sacred and the secular, as they present themselves to-day, by way of showing how each is incomplete and unsatisfying in itself, and each is in need of the other in a full orbed view of human life. There on the one hand is the world of preoccupation with external interests and pursuits. Such pre-eminently is the world of Western civilisation, with its absorption in creative activity, in the conquest of nature and the harnessing of natural forces for human use. For Western society, taken as a whole, this is the one thing that matters, which engages our energies and holds our interest. We are bent on building for ourselves by the aid of science a secure and ever-securer home within the visible order. Very largely our world is the world of industry and commerce. Our best efforts and thought are given to improved methods of production and distribution. We measure our success by the quantity of goods that issues from our hands and is placed on the markets of the world. Our highest admiration goes out to feats of conquest over the natural elements, to mechanical inventions by which barriers of time and space are overcome, and sea, land and air are brought under our sway. Look in what direction we may, we are confronted with domains of human activity of absorbing interest, so absorbing as to exclude all else. These secular interests and pursuits have emancipated themselves from all external control, and go their own way as if not merely were they made for man but man was made for them. Yet this very absorption in the external world carries with it its own inherent peril. The very achievements of man's skill may well become his own undoing. The world of invention and machinery bids fair to master its own creator. It tends to become his prison instead of his home; and man finds himself increasingly forced into the moulds of the artificial world of his own making. Living wholly in and for his secular pursuits, they set their mark upon him : and because of its total exclusion of the other world which has an equal claim on his attention, his life emerges from the process starved and stunted, and is lived within limits which forbid the attainment of its own fulness and perfection.

For all the time over against the secular world, the world of absorption in the external and material, is the other world, that of spiritual realities and things unseen and eternal, the world with which the East, and particularly India, is primarily concerned, so much so that in comparison with it the external world is regarded as unreal and illusory. Here is the domain of religion, which on its side, too, in modern life is apt to go its own way without regard to and often in marked antagonism to secular interests. Sometimes, indeed, the recoil from an unduly mechanistic and materialistic outlook takes the form of an equally exaggerated extreme on the spiritual side, of denying the reality of the material, of claiming that all that is is pure spirit. Yet short of this extremer tendency religion in its organised forms is apt to be regarded, and sometimes to regard itself, as a separate and specialised department of human interests, of concern to those only whose interest is drawn that way, and who are not usually actively interested in the world of external activity : and there is apt to be mutual distrust, if not contempt, on the part of those on one side of the line and those of the other. Yet religion and the domain of the spiritual suffers equally with secular interests from being isolated and confined within a department of its own. It tends to evaporate into a thin and emasculated piety through lack of bracing contact with the outward and visible world. For that world is presented to it not to condemn, to exclude or to hold at arm's length, but to interpret, to penetrate and to subdue : and so long as the spiritual holds itself apart in rigid aloofness from the external, so long will it lack that content and expression which is necessary for it, if it is to play its due part in a life individual and social which is satisfying and complete.

Thus the two spheres of human interest and pursuit confront each other, largely in isolation from and in contrast with each other, yet each with its rightful claim to recognition and inclusion in a life which is complete : and just as for the individual a life in which his external and spiritual interests are kept in rigidly separate compartments is divided against itself, and hence is incomplete and unsatisfy ing, so on the broad stage of modern civilisation the way must be found of reconciliation between the apparently conflicting claims of the sacred and the secular, if unity and completeness are to characterise life as a whole. It is the contention of these lectures that in the Incarnation and the religion of the Incarnation alone is the antithesis between the two worlds resolved and a satisfying way of unity found. For in Christ, God and man, the two worlds of the outward and the inward, the spiritual and the material, of eternity and time, meet and blend in a sacramental unity. The Incarnation is the seal and pledge of a unity within which the sacred and the secular are each given full recognition, but no longer in separation from one another. In Christ the two spheres commonly held apart are seen to interpenetrate, interpret and complete each other. On the one hand the world of nature and of the conquest of nature by human skill is seen in its spiritual significance, and as subordinated to spiritual ends : and on the other the world of religion and of unseen and eternal reality becomes the supremely effective factor in the shaping of human life through contact with the manifold interests and activities of man which it is set to interpret and to hallow.

It is the sacramental principle, supremely illustrated in the Incarnation, which as applied to the world as a whole can alone provide a satisfying way of reconciliation and unity. By the sacramental principle is affirmed that neither the material nor the spiritual is complete in itself, but each needs the other for its completion; the outward and visible only coming to its own when subdued and penetrated by the spiritual, and the spiritual remaining inchoate and nebulous unless finding a visible vehicle of expression. The rigid line often drawn between the sacred and the secular, drawn as sharply from the side of religion as from that of everyday life, involves a false distinction. Certainly it is not true to the genius of Christianity : for it is Christianity, the religion of the Incarnation, which is unique in this, that in spite of constant pressure it has consistently refused to condemn the outward and the natural as inherently lacking in spiritual worth and value : while with equal consistency it has proclaimed the insufficiency and incompleteness of the outward and the natural within their own limits and on their own level. It proclaims in Christ the union of God with man, and through man the union of God with all that world of nature and the visible order which forms the environment of human life and the principle scene of human activity. In the light of the Incarnation and its extension in the sacramental order, the discord is resolved, and whether in the individual life or in that of society, outward and inward, sacred and secular, religion and external interests, can each find its rightful scope in relation to the other. The world of external interests and activity demands its full recognition as a rightful sphere of human energy, yet remains incomplete, indeed, frustrates and crushes humanity itself, unless it is brought under law to Christ, and in Christ is charged with spiritual significance. The world of religion has, too, its indefeasible claim, a claim, moreover, which only then is fully satisfied when it has found expression and manifestation in the external world, and has penetrated and subdued it by the Spirit of Christ.

It is the concluding task of these lectures to relate what has been written on the Incarnation in connection with modern thought and life to the Anglican tradition, and to suggest that in the task of reconciling sacred and secular, of bringing all orders of human interest and activity under the dominion of Christ, the Anglican Church has both a responsibility and an opportunity all her own. It is indeed our contention that in her outlook, her teaching, her worship, the Anglican Church has been true to primitive Catholic tradition in safeguarding and applying those values for which, we have seen, the Incarnation stands. This is not to deny that there have been long periods during which the sense of her Catholic character and mission has been lost and she has grievously failed to bear her rightful witness in the world. Yet it is, as we shall endeavour to show, precisely at those epochs of her history in modern times when she has been most conscious of herself and of her place in Christendom, and has endeavoured to give that consciousness most clear and articulate expression, that this very characteristic of loyalty to the truth of the Incarnation and its implications has emerged most unmistakably into view : and while it is no part of our task to criticise other communions, we may yet make bold to assert that in her capacity for balance and proportion of view, of allowing in teaching and practice for all sides and aspects of the truth, for that Catholicity which consists of regard for all those values that must be taken into account in the divine economy of redemption, the Anglican Church occupies a place of special importance among the communions of the Christian world. Such gifts, if she possess them, are not hers to claim as a monopoly, but to use to the full and to bestow freely for the benefit of the whole body and for the better discharge of the mission of the Catholic Church in the world.

The earlier stages of the Reformation epoch in England were no sooner over than the Church found herself compelled to think out her position and to assert it for her own satisfaction and in defence against external aggression. The accession of Elizabeth in 1558 was the beginning of a period, lasting for a full century, during which the Church of England was beset on two sides and was forced to contend for and to formulate a reasoned position of her own which could hold its ground and justify itself against rival theories of religion and the Church. She had on the one hand to justify her refusal to submit to the Rome and the Papacy of the counter-Reformation. For it must be remembered that on the Roman as well as on the Anglican side, mediæval theory and practice had passed, had indeed become an acknowledged anachronism: and it was not so much the Rome of the Middle Ages, as the Rome which emerged from the Council of Trent, which the Anglican Church, as other communions, had and has to take into account: a Rome in which the conciliar conception of authority could find no place, in which the Papacy was entrenched in a position of unquestioned predominance such as overrode all other and lesser organs of expression and found its logical outcome in the dogma of 1870: a Rome, further, in which doctrines were defined with a sharpness and precision of language, largely borrowed from scholastic theology, which excluded their re-statement in terms of new knowledge. It was against such a conception and assertion of centralised authority and against its arbitrary exercise, that the Anglican Church was and is a standing protest. Yet while repudiating papal authority as so defined, it was far from disowning the need and place of authority in matters of religion. The authority, however, for which it stood and stands is one which resides in the whole Church and finds its normal and traditional expression in a General or Œcumenical Council, when such may be held, or, under the circumstances of a divided Christendom, in local or regional Councils, representative, so far as may be, of the Church as a whole.

Yet equally had the Church of England to stand its ground against the even more aggressive claims of continental Protestantism. In her reaction against the Papal system of authority and jurisdiction, the natural, indeed the logical course, of the English Church would have been to go the whole length of the continental Reformers, and with Papal authority to have repudiated that whole ancient order, of ministry, creed and liturgy, which appeared to be bound up with it. For a century attacks were made and pressed home on the episcopate and on the liturgy in favour of a new ministry, and a new order of worship and discipline founded on the word of Scripture without regard to Catholic tradition. The utmost pressure was brought to bear upon the Church to align herself with the Calvinistic models set up at Geneva and elsewhere. Such attempts were resisted and failed in face of an instinct which went far deeper than can be explained on any grounds of political expediency. Undoubtedly political considerations entered largely into the Elizabethan settlement, in its rejection of Papal obedience on the one hand and Puritanic individualism or congregationalism on the other. Undoubtedly the refusal of one and the other was in part at least the outcome of the imperative need of national unity. Yet out of the turmoil and strife of the times Elizabeth builded greater than she knew : and there gradually emerged into view a conception of the English Church, which both marked it off clearly from other and more logical systems on either side, and gave it a positive character of its own.

Such was the outcome of events. But before the close of the sixteenth century the necessity arose of a clear formulation of that central position which the course of events rather than deliberate design had assigned to the English Church, and of its justification on grounds other than those of immediate expediency. " If the religion of the Prayer Book was to remain supreme, it was necessary to justify it by reason as well as to enforce it by law, and a new and systematic theology was required for the purpose." [2] For the Church the necessity was pressing for " a review of her whole doctrinal and historical position in the light of the Reformation." [3] In Richard Hooker, who published the first four books of his *Laws of Ecclesiastical Polity* in 1594, a scholar and writer appeared who sought to justify and succeeded in justifying the position of the English Church by the threefold appeal to reason, history and learning. In a real measure the English Church and Hooker as its interpreter succeeded where Erasmus had failed : for it was Erasmus' dream " to unite the spirit of humanism with that of

[2] *History of the Church of England:* Wakeman, p. 349.
[3] *op. cit.*

Christianity, and to substitute for a scholastic, dogmatic, monastic, ascetic Christianity, what he called
the Philosophy of Christ." [4]   Hooker's defence was
indeed mainly directed to the outlook and claims of
Puritanism rather than those of Rome. And equally
with Erasmus and the Humanists did he insist on
finding in religion room for all those values of life,
all the interests and activities which are the natural
fruit of the spirit of man.

It was here that the rigid exclusive ultra-logical
discipline of Presbyterian Protestantism, as it took
shape in the seventeenth century, so wholly failed
to satisfy the spiritual needs of the English people.
" It was incompatible with a genial and liberal
humanism which recognises the virtues as well as the
vices of human nature, accepts pleasure itself as a
good, and recognises in the arts, whatever their aber-
rations, the fullest expression of man's sense of
values." [5]   So long as this religious regime was
dominant and was backed by the strong arm of the
State, the arts were driven underground or at
least were relegated to the sphere of the world,
the flesh and the devil which religion was to
keep at arm's length. The drama [6] and music were
condemned, and a Shakespeare was forced by the
temper of the times to be " content with the rôle of

---

[4] *Cross-currents in English Literature of the Seventeenth
Century:* Grierson, p. 17.

[5] *op. cit.,* p. 191.

[6] cp. Prynne : *Histriomastix* (quoted Grierson, *op. cit.,* p. 71).
" All popular and common plays are such sinful, lustful and
pernitious recreations as are altogether unseemly, and unlaw-
ful unto Christians."

purveying amusement for Court and populace."[7] Nor did the thought occur " why so potent an instrument as the stage might not be enlisted in the service of a purer religion and ethics."[8] A rigid moral discipline was enforced in which the main emphasis was laid on the " restrictive virtues "[9] to the exclusion of the " more positive and outgoing spirit "[10] of the Christian temper. The primary doctrines preached and inculcated were those of predestination and imputed righteousness. S. Paul, or one aspect of S. Paul's teaching, was pressed to the disparagement of the humanist spirit of the Gospels, and human nature was forced from its proper course by the supposed demands of an all-dominant religion. The peril of such an unnatural regime was that of an excessive recoil of human passion and desire, once the yoke was removed; such a recoil as indeed marked the period of the Restoration. It was now however that the true character of the Anglican Church was revealed as in line with that primitive Catholicism, Eastern rather than Western, which saw in Christianity the redemption and consecration of human life in its full range and expression. The English Church stood out as the " champion of spiritual freedom."[11] Hooker, as we have seen, gave her a philosophical basis and defended the priceless treasures of the human spirit, reason, history and learning, from the tyranny of the eternal decrees. On another plane the work of Hooker was taken up

[7] Grierson, *op. cit.*

[8] Grierson, *op. cit.*

[9] Grierson, *op. cit.*, p. 31.

[10] Grierson, *Ib.*, p. 31.

[11] Grierson, *op. cit.*, p. 204.

and carried on by poets such as Herbert and Vaughan with their emphasis on the " humanist aspect of Christianity." The former particularly, " the most characteristic Anglican," in his life as in his writings revealed how the works of man, the toil of the labourer, as much as the achievements of the artist and the scholar, could be redeemed for God, and how the round of the Christian year as preserved and simplified in the Prayer Book gave the opportunity of relating to Christ and to religion the recurring activities and routines of everyday life. Thus, as interpreted by her theologians and poets, and as lived in the lives of her faithful sons, a type of religion emerged as the characteristic outcome of the Anglican standpoint which was true to the principles and values of the Incarnation, and was capable of a deepening and extension such as would render it applicable to the fuller and more complicated life of later times.

If we pass direct from the Reformation epoch of the sixteenth and seventeenth centuries, and the outlook and mind which emerged from that period as characteristic of the Anglican Church, to the Oxford or Tractarian Movement of the nineteenth century, it is not because the intervening period had not its own interest and value for religion and its own contribution to make in the sphere of religion. It is, however, in the main true that during the eighteenth century and the early part of the nineteenth, the English Church suffered, along with other communions, a spiritual eclipse which hid from itself and from the world its true character, and under which it

largely lost the sense of the transcendent element in
religion, and, protected and patronised by the State,
sank into an institution for the maintenance of the
existing social and moral order. It is true that with
the Wesleyan and Evangelical Movements a spiritual
awakening occurred which brought religion home
to the common people and gave to the Church a
succession of saintly characters of whom she may be
justly proud. Yet the Movement failed, for indeed
it did not seek, to quicken into life the corporate
consciousness of the Church, or the sense of her
historic place and mission in Catholic Christendom
and the world as a whole : and it was left to the
founders and leaders of the Oxford Movement, the
centenary of the beginning of which is shortly to be
celebrated, to take up and carry forward under new
and very different conditions the work which the
scholars and saints of the seventeenth century had
attempted to do. By their work of preaching and
lecturing, by the issue of tracts, some mere leaflets,
others considerable treatises, by making known
through translation the patristic writings they sought
to awaken the mind of the Church to her historic
and apostolic character and to the supernatural order
of grace of which she was the divinely ordained
guardian and channel.

Emerging from the cloisters of a university and
originated by its scholars, the Movement had from
the first an intellectual quality through which it was
able to base the claims of the English Church on that
appeal to sound learning, which, as we have seen,
was one of the main notes struck by the Anglican

divines of the seventeenth century : and it is in no small measure due to their work, in the historical and theological spheres, that the English Church occupies, in the recognition of others as well as of her own sons, that place of opportunity and service which is hers in the Christian world of to-day. Yet the primary emphasis of the early leaders of the Movement was on the moral rather than the intellectual side of religion. A recent writer on the subject speaks of " that aspiration after personal holiness, and dissatisfaction with failure to attain it, which was the very soul of the piety cultivated by the Oxford teachers." [12] So far from being primarily concerned with the externals of religion, and its ceremonial aspect, it was on inwardness that they laid most stress and upon a moral purity based upon a supernaturally imparted grace. Perhaps, however, their principal service was to revive and give shape to an organic and corporate conception of religion and of the Church in striking contrast with the almost exclusive stress on individual salvation which was characteristic of evangelical piety. That the Church is a body with its own life and law of growth, a society ministering on earth yet of divine origin, its episcopate and priesthood the God-given channels of its service to men, with its own polity and government not subject to civil or political control, yet claiming itself to sanctify and subdue to Christ the whole man and the whole order of human society, such were among the truths which were

[12] *Religious Thought in the Oxford Movement:* C. C. J. Webb, p. 53.

L

brought into fresh light by the teachers of the movement : and the teaching so given increasingly received practical application through the rise of a new
conception of priestly character and service finding
an outlet in the parochial life of the crowded industrial centres of England.

In contrast again with the evangelical revival it
was the Incarnation rather than the Atonement on
which the Tractarian Movement laid primary stress :
and with that change of emphasis in the sphere of
doctrine went a change of religious outlook and of
the content of religious experience. It was, as we
have seen, the assurance of personal salvation
through the vicarious sacrifice of Christ, and the
experience known as conversion, which for evangelical thought was not only the foundation of the
religious structure for the individual life, as indeed
it is, but came to be regarded as the norm and
standard and test of true religion. The result was
a tendency to ignore and disparage qualities moral
and spiritual which could not be brought under the
heading of this standard type of experience. On
the one hand, in the sphere of natural religion apart
from the Christian revelation, little value was
attached to gifts and qualities and virtues there
found, as capable of being brought into the service
of Christ : and on the other hand, equally little was
made of the higher types of holiness, of the process
of sanctification through sacramental grace, and of
that life of special consecration to which some at
least might be called.

Over against this stress on a particular form

of spiritual experience, a re-emphasising of the Incarnation as the central doctrine of the Christian revelation brought with it not only a new conception of the Church, in its organic and corporate capacity, but a vastly increased range of the scope and content of religious experience. For the Incarnation, as has again and again been pointed out in these lectures, carries with it by implication the hallowing of human nature and life, and of all that is proper to it, by contact with the divine. And in laying stress upon this, as for it the central truth of revelation, the Oxford and Catholic Movement within the Church of England carried with it at least by implication a new conception of the place of religion and of the mission of the Church. It made its appeal to the whole man, and recognised the capacity for redemption and sanctification of the natural virtues and qualities of humanity and of the whole range of human activity : and by regaining for the Eucharist that place of central importance in Christian devotion and worship which it rightly occupies, its leaders and representatives brought into fresh light the largely forgotten truth of the sacramental order and the sacramental principle as fundamental to the right understanding and application of the truth of the sovereignty of Christ over the whole domain of human life.

The truths, then new and revolutionary, when rediscovered and proclaimed by the earlier leaders of the Oxford Movement, of the Incarnation, the Church, the Priesthood and the Sacraments, as inseparable links in the main chain of Christian revelation, have now won general acceptance and recognition, from those, included, who would regard themselves as heirs of the evangelical tradition : and the acceptance and application of these truths has meant for the English Church a new and vastly extended scope and mission undreamed of in earlier periods. The Oxford Movement was mainly valuable in the sphere of ideas, of proclaiming afresh fundamental truths of the Catholic religion, which, however far forgotten, were yet an essential element of the Anglican tradition. Its leaders largely left it to later generations to carry into action and practice the ideas and truths so taught. It was only slowly and with many set-backs that the lump could be leavened, and the seed so sown bear its fruit. Yet the recent history of the English Church, or rather of the Anglican Communion, has shown that those values and implications of the truth of the Incarnation, on which stress has been laid in these lectures, have received wide recognition and expression. It reveals, too, that in the great task of to-day, already alluded to, of redeeming for Christ the secular order of society and civilisation, the English Church has through its Catholic inheritance, coupled with its spiritual freedom, a part of pre-eminent importance to play.

In two directions illustrations of this truth are ready to hand. In her missionary enterprise the English Church has laid increasing stress on the differing gifts and qualities possessed by peoples and races, and which are there not to be suppressed or rejected but brought in and exercised as contributory to the fulness of Christ. It has long been recognised that it is not the aim of the missionary and of the Church's missionary agencies to impress on native peoples a uniform stamp of religious expression, whether in worship or in life, but to encourage as wide a variety as possible of character and devotion, personal and corporate, subject to the common recognition of the essentials of Catholic faith and order. Not reproductions of the English Church, but native churches rooted in the soil of national and racial life, within which the native genius for religion may find its proper scope, and within which all that belongs to the people of culture and occupation and life can, subject to conformity with the law of Christ, be brought within the sphere of its religious life and its sacramental worship, such is the missionary aim, and such increasingly the missionary achievement of the English Church. It builds on what is there, recognises and appraises at their true worth all that is of value in native religion, culture and custom, and, while demanding as the price of Christian profession and baptism an utter repudiation of that which is avowedly evil and demonic in native belief and life, seeks to bring into obedience to Christ, and so to carry to full fruition, the capacities which are already present : and corresponding with this aim and method its conception of the Anglican communion as a whole, indeed by implication of the Catholic Church, is that of a unity qualified by the richest diversity, of churches knit together by the common bonds of faith and order, yet self-governing within their own limits, con-

tributing and receiving those treasures of Christian
life, fellowship and devotion which offered from
many sides are there for the enrichment of the
whole body and every part of it.

A similar principle is seen at work in the approach
to Reunion which is now characteristic of the Church
of England. Here, again, it is recognised that separate communions, whatever the historical origin of
the separation, have developed in isolation certain
gifts of piety and devotion, of character and worship, which are of value, but which, as such, are the
rightful possession not of one communion only, but
of the whole Church. It is no longer asserted or
claimed that any one church represents that normal
and regulative standard to which all others must
conform, if reunion is to be achieved. It no longer
looks to absorption as the way of unity. Here, too,
as in the missionary sphere, it looks for and wel-
comes a wide variety and diversity as not contrary
to but characteristic of the unity which it seeks.
Certain common marks of the Church, a common
faith, a common ministry, and common sacraments,
these it recognises as essential features of a united
church. But within these limits it looks for a wide
measure of group liberty, a wide variety of forms of
devotion and worship, to a large extent the retention
of existing group affiliations within the united body :
and the ideal which it contemplates is, to quote the
words of the Lambeth Appeal of 1920, " a Church
genuinely Catholic, loyal to all truth, and gathering
into its fellowship all who profess and call themselves Christians, within whose visible unity all the

treasures of faith and order, bequeathed as a heritage by the past to the present, shall be possessed in common, and made serviceable to the whole Body of Christ."

Here, then, are two examples of the application of the principle, inherent in the truth and religion of the Incarnation, of providing full scope for human values and expressions of the human spirit, while yet bringing these into contact with and under the sovereignty of the divine. They are illustrated further in that wide sweep and variety of subjects which recent Lambeth Conferences have taken into cognisance, industry, international relationships, marriage and sex. The consideration of these and cognate subjects, and pronouncements upon them, go to show that in increasing measure the Church is taking as its province and sphere of redemptive activity the whole order of modern society and every range and department of human interest and activity, and regards its task, a task indeed which can only be fulfilled as it is faced by the Catholic Church as one, as that of bringing into obedience to Christ all men and the totality of human life.

One last word. We kneel before the altar as the Holy Eucharist is offered and the Blessed Sacrament of Christ's Body and Blood is bestowed. There in a very real sense is the miracle of the Incarnation ever renewed. For there inseparably conjoined in sacramental unity is heaven and earth, the temporal and the eternal, the spiritual and the bodily. There, in making the common gifts of bread and wine the vehicles and channels of His most sacred Presence,

Christ by implication takes to Himself and redeems and sanctifies human nature and human life, body and soul alike, and indeed the whole order of nature which shares with humanity the capacity for redemption.   There, too, as we offer these gifts in the Holy place, we present by implication, indeed by open avowal, ourselves, our souls and bodies to be a "reasonable, holy and living sacrifice," and together with ourselves we bring for acceptance at the altar, and into union with Christ, all that is of humanity and the world of man.   There ourselves, and all mankind, all that is proper to human nature and life, all spheres of human interest, pursuit, activity, find a place in our act of consecration, and are taken up into the Holies to find their crown and consummation through union with the Divine.

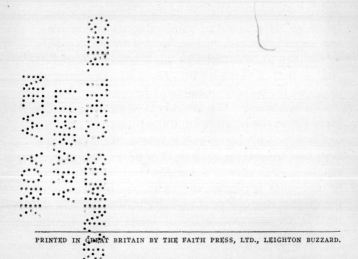

PRINTED IN GREAT BRITAIN BY THE FAITH PRESS, LTD., LEIGHTON BUZZARD.